# END
# FEMINISM
# SAVE
# THE
# WORLD

First Printing: September 2014

Revised December 2018

ISBN: 978-1501074332

PYXIS PUBLISHING
Salt Lake City, Utah

*To all the valiant mothers who've chosen to sacrifice a career and worldly accolades for the eternal blessings of a family.*

# CONTENTS

# INTRODUCTION

WE'RE just trying to save the world. No one can deny it: our world needs saving. All you have to do is turn on the news, step outside, or even look within the walls of your own home to witness a fraction of our crumbling society. Crime is running rampant; poverty is on the rise; depression, anxiety, and mental illness are household issues. Abuse is far too common; divorce plagues us; drug addiction, alcoholism, pornography, and other types of addiction are bigger epidemics than we ever predicted. We're in trouble.

In our desperation for a better world, we look to politicians. We look to world leaders. We demand new legislation and social reform. We boycott and protest and riot and throw money at causes. We seek out big picture solutions to solve these big picture problems.

But this isn't the answer. Like most big picture problems, the answer is much closer to home than any of us realize. In fact, the answer is *inside* the home. The answer is the family.

I challenge you to think of a single social ill in the world that can't be traced back to a lack of a healthy family structure. The family is an immensely powerful force for good or for evil; its influence ripples throughout the community and lingers for generations. It can create a tremendous amount of strength or it can be the cause of one's downfall.

If the answer is the family, how then do we strengthen this fundamental building block of society? How do we stop this destructive cycle of broken homes?

We believe a large part of that solution is to allow women to be women. Or in other words, allow women to be the glue that holds families together and the powerful influence for good they were always designed to be—an influence of which modern-day feminism has largely indoctrinated out of women. This book is our case that the modern-day feminist movement has mutated the female race almost beyond recognition. Luckily, we women have the unique ability to turn things around, to repair the family, to take back our power.

Before I lose you, I want to make it clear that this book is not anti-woman by a long shot. In fact, you may never read a more pro-woman book in your life (or pro-man for that matter). But as women, we've felt a profound sense that most feminist causes are not at all pro-woman. Instead, they seek to destroy femininity by squashing natural female characteristics in favor of masculine ones, and they likewise destroy masculinity by shouting men into silence and submission. Feminism throws society into an unnatural imbalance. A feminist cannot be an egalitarian because the word itself inherently elevates the wellbeing of one gender over another. Masculinism, or what the Internet has dubbed "meninism," has the same effect on the opposite side. Neither feminism nor meninism recognize the complementary reliance of women and men on each other.

As we've seen throughout much of history, an excess of masculinism will produce negative consequences on society such as disrespect for women and a failure to see the value in women. However, an excess of feminism produces a society who devalues men, a female race who seeks to hijack the male roles of society, and women who no longer wish to marry or have children. Worse, it produces women who view children as mere parasites who ought to be avoided or aborted. Both feminism and masculinism seem determined to prove that they can do it on their own without being tied down to the opposite gender. Both mindsets are equally destructive to the family structure. Because of that, this book could be titled "End Masculinism; Save the World," and it would be just as accurate.

However, masculinism isn't the biggest threat of today, so we won't address it much in this book. I acknowledge that in the past masculinism reigned supreme and many women were oppressed and disrespected under it. This was wrong. But when society attempts to correct itself, the pendulum often swings too far in the other direction. Feminism is nothing more than the opposite side of the same destructive coin. Complementarianism--or the idea that women are great, men are great, but together we're *really* great--is what we should seek instead. Societal balance between the male and female is what creates a healthy foundation for families. The best way to achieve that balance is through marriage between a man and a woman.

Who are you? You're the reader who bought this book to either 1) scorn and mock, 2) validate what you already believe, or 3) to attempt to learn something new with an open mind to opinions that may not fit with your previously held beliefs. I sincerely hope you fall into the third category. This isn't about left or right, young or old, Pepsi or Coke. It's about truth. We hope you'll be a truth-seeking reader. We'll try to be the same kind of writers.

Who are we? We're a mother and daughter team who strongly feel the urge to contribute to the solution rather than the problem. We're going to tell you what we know—what we've learned from personal experience, our trusty female intuition, and endless amounts of research. Whether or not you agree with what we have to say, we believe we have a moral obligation to share this information. Take it or leave it.

We're just trying to save the world.

# 1

## WE'VE ALWAYS HAD POWER

WOMEN have the power to change the world. Whether for good or for evil, women have held this power since the dawn of time. The earliest recorded example of womanhood is evidence of this. Don't believe it? Just pull out that dusty Bible and reread the book of Genesis. In the beginning, God created woman's power. He knew Adam couldn't do it alone. He needed a complement—a driving force to help him improve—to help him become the best man he could be. And God knew the only way for Adam to be complete, to truly progress, was to have a wife. So He created Eve—His final and crowning creation, the first woman in a very long line of amazing women who would be the necessary strength and support system behind every amazing man who would ever live. And not just a support to others, but powerful in her own right; powerful in a different way.

In Genesis 2:18 God says, "It is not good that the man should be alone; I will make him an help meet for him."

*Help meet* is a term that much of the modern world has defined as an assistant, helper, or even servant. This couldn't be further from the truth. The meaning of the original Hebrew word for *help meet*, or *ezer k'enegdo*, means something very different. In Diana Webb's book, *Forgotten Women of God*, she explains:

> The noun ezer occurs 21 times in the Hebrew Bible. In eight of these instances the word means "savior." These examples are easy to identify because they are associated with other expressions of deliverance or saving. Elsewhere in the Bible, the root ezer means "strength".... the word is most frequently used to describe how God is an ezer to man.

The second half of this term, *k'enegdo*, has been translated as *fit for*, *meet for*, or *worthy of*. Some have understood *k'enegdo* to mean *exactly corresponding to*, or a mirror image. Not above, not below, but equal to.

When we put these two words together, *ezer k'enegdo*, we have a role vastly more powerful than what

2

we've come to understand as a "help meet." We could instead translate it as "a savior to man who is equal to man."

God wasn't the only one who understood Eve's power. If you'll notice, when the serpent realized he couldn't tempt Adam to partake of the forbidden fruit, he chose to tempt Eve instead. Why? Because Satan is cunning. He knew Eve was the most influential person in Adam's life—possibly even more influential than God himself—and the serpent knew he would be most effective by corrupting Eve first. He knew she held the power within her hands to change the very fabric of the world. And the serpent was right. With one single act, Eve changed the world forever. Whether for better or for worse, depending on your personal religious views, it's a virtually undeniable fact that Eve, a woman, was the first leader the world ever knew. And interestingly enough, Adam, a man, was the first follower.

Now, if the Bible isn't your number one source for history or belief, then the pile of examples of other amazing, world-changing women should rekindle those nightmares about Joan of Arc squashing Jupiter with her pinky finger. Anne Frank, Sacagawea, Rosa Parks, Mother Teresa, Florence Nightingale, Harriet Tubman, Cory Ten Boom, the list goes on. These are women who achieved greatness, not *despite* their femininity, but as a direct result of their uniquely feminine characteris-

3

tics. Traits such as meekness, charity, spirituality, compassion, humility, sacrifice, selflessness, creativity, and so on.

This is why the ridiculous notion that women never had any power before the all-important feminist movement saved the female race, is just that: ridiculous. Women don't need, and never have needed, any help being powerful. To suggest women need a militant movement, shouting from the rooftops that we're just as good as men, is nothing more than insulting. It seems that women who truly understand their worth shouldn't need to shove it down everyone's throats or, even more ironically, feel the need to warp the whole gender into something that's no longer feminine at all.

This isn't to say women have always been valued the way we should have been. There were many legitimate needs for the early feminist movement such as: securing a woman's right to vote, ensuring we were granted the same opportunities as men, and fighting against legitimate injustices. These injustices are of particular concern in areas like the Middle East, where women are still suffering under all kinds of oppression.

Oddly enough, the feminist movement as a whole is virtually silent on the sufferings of *those* women— women who fall victim to real crimes such as honor killings, rape, abuse, and the 125 million women around the world who are forced to endure female genital mutilation. Think about the enormity of that number for a minute. That's almost the number of *all* women living in the United States right now. But instead of helping those women rise above the violence and empower themselves, feminists use their voice and influence to demand free birth control, to insist upon their "right" to kill their unborn children, to do anything within their power to create consequence-free promiscuity and immodesty, to degrade and emasculate men, to appropriate the male life path, to fight against the illusory "gender wage-gap," to persecute other women who do anything inherently female, and to whine. A lot.

The most perplexing part about the feminist movement is the group of people we call Gender Blenders, or the so-called feminists who seem to think the best way to empower women is to make them *not* women at all. Sure, women can *look* like women (sometimes), but they're required to *act* like men, otherwise they're nothing special—a concept that, when it comes to a movement that claims to celebrate womanhood, is a total contradiction.

It's obvious that a career woman is the "ideal" woman by the world's standards today. It doesn't matter how much her family is going to pot at home or how deeply miserable she is on the inside, as long as she has a fancy desk, parking space, and all the external accolades from society. "Super mom," they call her.

"She can do it all." "She's teaching her daughters how to be strong and independent." But a homemaker? "Wow, she must be so oppressed." "She must not be good at anything." "What does she do all day?" "She probably couldn't handle a *real* job." "She must be an inbred hillbilly or a religious zealot."

Since the beginning of civilization, women have held roughly the same familial role: nurturing, caretaking, child-bearing and rearing, taking care of the domestic work and the home front while the men were away at work or war. This was the basic role of women for thousands of years, regardless of race, culture, or part of the world. Then, almost in an instant, it changed. It was less than a hundred years ago that things were turned on their head. Think about that. In less than a hundred years—more specifically since World War II, the entire female race became something wildly different. Feminists will tell you this is a good thing. They like to take credit for "liberating" women and earning women the "privilege" of entering the workforce. But even that's not entirely true. Women originally entered the workforce, not because of feminist influence and not because they wanted to, but out of necessity due to so many men being drafted in the 1940s. This new idea that all women should leave their families for the sake of a career, something feminists promote and celebrate, is really just a lingering aftereffect from one of the world's most devastating wars. When you get right down to it, the argument could be made that Hitler is more responsible for starting the female career lifestyle than feminists are, though they're most certainly to blame for keeping it alive today.

In our generation, it may feel like these career expectations for women have been around forever, but in the grand scheme of human history, they're only a blip on the radar. And if we begin to wake up, it's completely possible for us as a human race to move back to what we instinctually know is the truth—that women and men are *different*.

This may be an obvious notion to some, but it's becoming increasingly less obvious to the world at large. Men and women are different. Just spend a little time in a middle school cafeteria and you'll be plenty convinced. But we know this purely on a scientific level. We've always been *equal* but also *different*, not just physically but mentally, spiritually, and emotionally. Take a few minutes to Google "men's vs. women's brains" and it should be clear we're meant for different natural roles.

Despite these differences, we're each equal in our value and importance to the world. This concept of "equal but different" is one many feminists have trouble with, so allow me to illustrate with an analogy about coins.

7

Take two quarters and five dimes for instance. Two quarters are equal to 50 U.S. cents, and so are five dimes. In other words, they're equal in monetary value and both will buy you approximately 1.2 inches of a Subway footlong. However, the coins themselves are far from the same. They differ in size, weight, depth, design, the presidents they honor, the writings engraved in them, the very metals they're composed of, and even the quantity. In other words, they're equal but different.

Trying to force two and a half dimes into a quarter mold won't make it a quarter. They're not made of the same basic stuff. Doing so will only destroy the dimes and diminish their value forever. Two quarters are always best at being two quarters and five dimes are always best at being five dimes. The same concept can be applied to men and women in their natural and God-given roles.

It's also worth noting, that together, two quarters and five dimes make a whole dollar. When men and women share their unique gifts with each other and join in marriage, they become what they can't become on their own. So go ahead and make that 2.4 inches of that footlong, ya crazy love birds.

If that doesn't speak to you, just look at the animal kingdom. Male and female animals from nearly every species have differing roles to play. Female lions, for example, are primarily responsible for feeding and car-ing for the cubs, while male lions are responsible for leading and protecting the pride. Male lions generally grow up and leave their pride to start their own, while lionesses stay with their pack for life. These are roles lions know inherently. No one has to teach them this.

Another example is the rhesus monkey. A fairly recent study performed by the Yerkes National Primate Center, concluded that male monkeys greatly preferred to play with toy trucks over dolls, while the female monkeys preferred dolls and soft, plushy animals. It's also common for female chimpanzees in the wild to play with sticks as though they were dolls. This is due to their developing maternal instinct.

We won't get into gender roles in relation to black widow spiders because ew. But you get the point. Even though animal gender roles vary greatly between species, it's obvious, no matter what species you look at, the roles are consistently *different* from one another. To force both sexes into the exact same mold is detrimental to any species. Can you imagine the widespread panic that would ensue among caretakers of animals if the two genders of penguins, for instance, suddenly became confused about their instinctual roles? What if *neither* gender in the emperor penguin species wanted to incubate the egg? What if they both decided, "Hey, I don't feel fulfilled. I'm just gonna leave this egg under a bush or something while I go 'find myself.' Is that

9

cool?" Extensive research and studies would begin immediately to find out why these poor animals were in such confusion that they didn't know how to be female or male any longer (the fact that they had learned to speak English might also be a cause for concern). Are they being poisoned? Is it global warming? Have they fallen ill to some horrible new penguin disease? The whole structure of their species would begin to fall apart. Any animal expert will tell you this. Gender roles are necessary for human beings as well as animals. Different roles, expectations, and responsibilities have created a well-oiled machine that has helped the human race survive and thrive until today.

Despite the illogical nature of it all, the goal of the modern feminist is to blend the genders to the point of unrecognition. This I-can-do-anything-a-man-can-do attitude not only confuses both genders, but puts unnecessary pressure on women, creating a generation of girls who think they have to be everything at once—a goal that's as devastating to a woman's mental health as it is utterly impossible.

The tried and true practice of traditional gender roles have kept families and civilization as a whole, thriving for millennia. Can we say the same thing about the modern-day family? Has the family structure ever been so fractured and muddled as it is now?

Think about this for a moment: if the serpent were to try to turn the world upside-down again today, don't you think womankind would be a primary target?

It's time to determine whether feminism is actually a poisonous snake lurking in the bushes. We need to take a good, hard look at the direction we're heading and be honest with ourselves—has it done more harm than good? It may be time we call a spade a spade and admit that feminism is not good for men, children, or women.

# 2

---

## LET'S TALK SEMANTICS

ONE of the most frustrating problems with feminism is the broadness of the term itself. The ambiguity of the word makes it difficult to discuss and easy to get lost in time-wasting arguments about semantics.

When I first began studying the world of feminism, I was under the incorrect impression that there were only two sides of the issue: feminism and anti-feminism.

After a lot of research and endless Internet debate, I realized there are an unbelievable number of facets on either side of the spectrum. No two feminists (or self-proclaimed anti-feminists, for that matter) seem to entirely agree with one another on the subject. Even more confusing is the fact that many of the issues on the feminist side completely contradict each other, something we'll talk about later.

The two authors of this book are highly opinionated, debate hardly new to us, but the issue of feminism sparks all kinds of heightened emotions we never could have imagined (from men and women alike). Everyone has their own customized view of what feminism actually means. That's a problem. For example: "reproductive rights" has become one of the biggest feminist causes in the modern day, but stances as far separated as being in favor of a woman's right to vote and being in favor of abortion are grouped under the same "feminist" umbrella, despite them being wildly different issues. Because of this, it's often assumed that those who support the Women's Rights Movement would naturally be pro-abortion as well. Since virtually every human being in the Western World supports the basic rights of women, such as voting rights and equal opportunities, it gives an unfair padding in numbers to a movement that also supports the termination of unborn life.

For this reason, I think it's important to break it down into separate groups. This is by no means all-inclusive, but these are the most common ideas within feminism and anti-feminism that we've encountered. Most people seem to belong to two or more of these factions, which only goes to show how divisive the movement has become. Please enjoy some charming doodles that illustrate this on the next page.

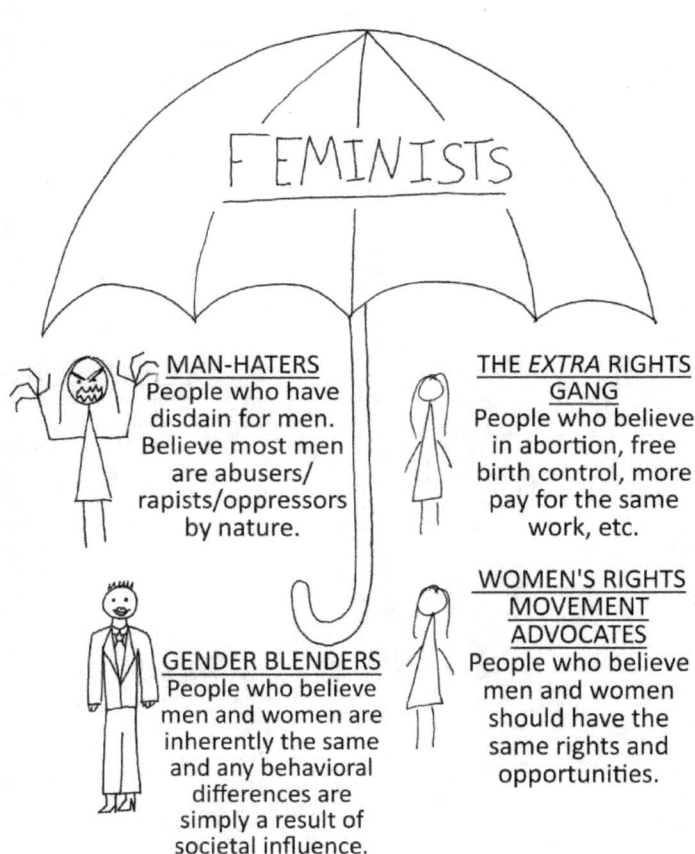

**FEMINISTS**

**MAN-HATERS**
People who have disdain for men. Believe most men are abusers/rapists/oppressors by nature.

**THE _EXTRA_ RIGHTS GANG**
People who believe in abortion, free birth control, more pay for the same work, etc.

**WOMEN'S RIGHTS MOVEMENT ADVOCATES**
People who believe men and women should have the same rights and opportunities.

**GENDER BLENDERS**
People who believe men and women are inherently the same and any behavioral differences are simply a result of societal influence.

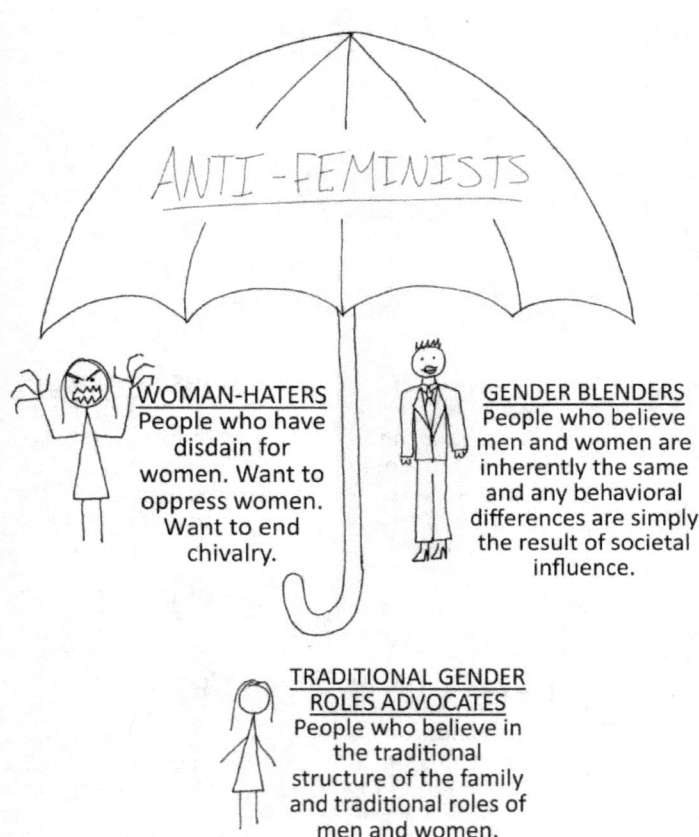

ANTI-FEMINISTS

**WOMAN-HATERS**
People who have disdain for women. Want to oppress women. Want to end chivalry.

**GENDER BLENDERS**
People who believe men and women are inherently the same and any behavioral differences are simply the result of societal influence.

**TRADITIONAL GENDER ROLES ADVOCATES**
People who believe in the traditional structure of the family and traditional roles of men and women.

16

As mentioned before, these were just the most common subcategories we came across and these are all likely to have many subcategories of their own.

Full disclosure: the authors of this book fall under two of these factions. We believe in equal rights *and* traditional gender roles. Yes, those ideas seem to be on separate sides of the aisle, which further illustrates the problem with how feminism has been organized, something we believe has been done intentionally to create a false dichotomy and promote damaging feminist beliefs.

For the sake of clarity, throughout the remainder of this book, when we refer to "feminism," we're referring to all the people who fall under the first three groups: the Man-Haters, The *Extra* Rights Gang, and the Gender Blenders—every piece of the feminist puzzle apart from the ideals of the Original Women's Rights Movement.

# 3

## FEMINISTS DON'T UNDERSTAND FEMINISM

H I. I'm a woman and I am not a feminist."
Saying this phrase anywhere on the Internet will inevitably get you the typical, "GASP. But don't you want the right to vote?" or "Some man in your life must be brainwashing you!" or "Way to spit on the graves of all the brave women who fought for your rights!"

The problem with debating someone who makes comments such as these is that it requires a history lesson that can't be contained in a snarky one-liner. So here goes.

### When Did Feminism Begin in the United States?

The answer to this question is complex. Most will tell you it began toward the beginning of the 20th Century, stemming from the Women's Suffrage Movement which secured a woman's right to vote. Their victory was solidified by the ratification of the 19th Amendment to the Constitution. But one truth many find difficult to swallow is this: Feminism isn't responsible for securing a woman's right to vote. Feminists usually attribute the earning of that right to the Women's Suffrage Movement or, what they now call "First-Wave Feminism." However, in those days, "suffragette" and "feminist" were not always one in the same. In fact, the term "feminist" was extremely rare in those days.

Google's Ngram Viewer, a chart that counts the number of times a word was used in literature over the years, shows that the word "feminism" was first introduced in the early 1900s, but at that time, it wasn't a common phrase by any means—it's barely a speed bump on the graph. The frequency of the word shot up out of nowhere in the 1960s and continued to grow until it peaked in the 90s.

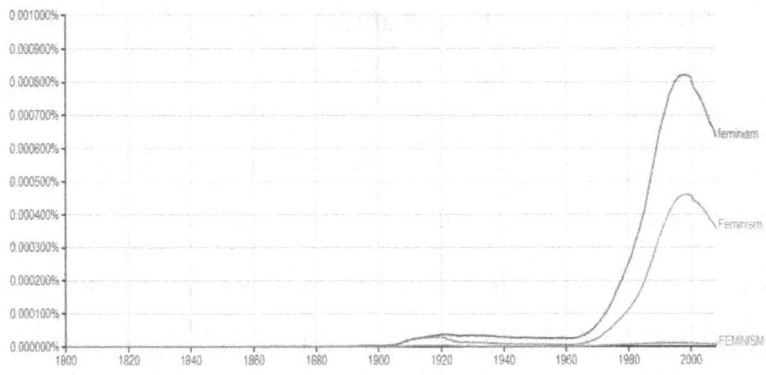

In other words, "First-Wave Feminism" is an invention of Third-Wave Feminism. And regardless of whether or not most Suffragettes were feminists, which is debatable, Suffragettes aren't solely responsible for securing a woman's right to vote either. Yes, they helped make leaps and bounds in the right direction, and we honor their work, but Suffragettes simply helped *restore* that right in *some* states. Many women held the right to vote in the United States as far back as the 1700s. Under the Constitution of the United States, voting right legislation was originally left up to the discretion of each individual state. In the days of our Founders, New York, Massachusetts, New Hampshire, and New Jersey allowed women to vote—way back when the entire male population was supposed to be sexist, right? Clearly all men weren't sexist, because men and women held equal voting rights, a law that could only have been implemented by men. The only requirement was that the voting woman owned land (and many did), which was a requirement for the men as well. Over time, this right was revoked for various political reasons. Politicians who couldn't secure the female vote felt they were at a disadvantage and fought to remove that right for their own selfish political gain. Others, including historian David Barton, have theorized that this right was revoked less on the grounds of sexism and more as an effort to preserve the family unit. In those days, voting was seen as a family matter. Rather than having each individual family member cast a vote, families were to come to a consensus and place one vote on behalf of the entire family, which the man, the head of the household, would then cast. Some felt that giving the husband, wife, and children the opportunity to vote differently could potentially tear families apart due to political disagreements. Thus, this right was eventually revoked.

William Bright, a saloonkeeper and member of his Wyoming city council, was the first to reintroduce women's voting rights. His bill passed in 1869. Yes, he was a man. Yes, those who voted in favor of his bill were also men. And yes, this was still 51 years before the 19th Amendment to the Constitution. Wyoming was closely followed the next year by Utah, which was only a territory and not yet a state at the time. In fact, 15 states allowed women the right to vote before the 19th Amendment was ratified.

This is in no way meant to diminish the work and suffering of the good women who fought in the Women's Suffrage Movement. Their work in regards to voting rights was commendable and necessary and we should be grateful. However, this fight began decades, even centuries before the Suffrage Movement was even a thought. And this fight for legitimate equality between the sexes began with those supposedly evil, sexist men.

## Feminists: Manipulated by Men Since 1929

While we're on the subject of the male influence on the women's movement, I think it's a good opportunity to dip into the flip side of this influence. Many feminists would likely be surprised and even mortified to learn that the first feminists in the United States were unknowingly and severely manipulated by the very men they were opposing.

During the First World War, President Woodrow Wilson appointed a man named Edward Bernays, nephew of psychoanalyst Sigmund Freud, to lead a massive propaganda campaign. The intention of this propaganda was to convince Europeans that America's war efforts would bring democracy and peace to Europe. While Wilson and Bernays visited Paris for a peace conference, they were stunned at the wild success they'd had on the minds of the people. Wilson's reception was one of admiration and adoration. The French were convinced that Wilson was a liberator, a powerful advocate for world freedom, even a hero. It was witnessing this eye-opening event that sparked an idea in the calculating mind of Edward Bernays.

"When I came back to the United States," Bernays said. "I decided that if you could use propaganda for war, you can certainly use it for peace. And 'propaganda' got to be a bad word because of the Germans using it, so what I did was to try and find some other words so we found the words 'council on public relations.'"

Under his new title, "public relations counselor," Edward Bernays began new experiments on the minds of the masses. These experiments included advertising campaigns with the purpose of persuading the collective to buy certain products. Some of his greatest success came in the form of manipulating feminists to start smoking cigarettes.

In the early 20th Century, it was a cultural taboo for women to smoke cigarettes, especially in public. It was considered a man's habit and a lady didn't participate. This was an obstacle for George Hill, then president of the American Tobacco Incorporation, since half of his potential customers were unreachable. To solve this problem, Hill sought the help of Edward Bernays and his propaganda expertise. Bernays took up the challenge and consulted with America's first psychoanalyst, Abraham Arden Brill, to discover what it would take to get women smoking like men. In their research and under heavy influence of Freud's methods, they found that women subconsciously viewed cigarettes as penises. Bernays saw the rise of feminism as the perfect opportunity to persuade women into smoking on the grounds that they were challenging male power with their own symbolic penises.

To carry out this mass persuasion, Bernays organized an unprecedented exhibition at New York's famous Easter Day Parade. He convinced a group of young, prominent women to hide cigarettes under their clothing and, at a signal given by him, they were to join the parade and dramatically light up. Bernays, beforehand, notified the press that there was to be a Suffragette protest during the parade and that the women were calling these cigarettes "Torches of Freedom."

From that moment on, the sale of "Torches of Freedom" amongst women skyrocketed. Smoking was seen as a symbol of independence and power. Though it didn't change any of these women's grievances, feminists were successfully convinced that smoking made them freer. These earliest feminists in the United States were manipulated by a group of men into developing a habit that today kills over 200,000 women a year. This false idea that smoking makes a woman more independent still lingers today considering almost half of all smokers are now women. Maybe worst of all, these early feminists were utterly convinced that choosing to smoke was *their* idea. These feminists a hundred years ago were under the impression that they were free-thinkers and trail blazers, but in actuality, they were simply tools used to increase the power of one conniving and greedy man. After hearing this story, it's more than reasonable to consider the possibility that each of us is being manipulated in other ways today, both as a collective and as individuals. Who is the Edward Bernays of our day, and how is he currently influencing the masses?

## Feminism's Second Wave

So, apart from bra-burning and hippies, what was the "Second-Wave of Feminism" about? Why did this begin? As we recall from the chart a few pages back, there was a massive spike in the term "feminism" in the 1960s. A woman's right to vote had been secured for decades, so what triggered this new dire need for a feminist movement? What was the huge injustice that sparked this mainstream discussion of feminism? Whatever the injustice was, it must have been even more outrageous than women being denied the right to vote. I mean, look at that slope!

Not exactly. This apparent injustice had virtually nothing to do with rights and everything to do with *culture*. The radical 1960s feminist movement was essentially a group of women who were unsatisfied with their own lives and decided to take it out on society. The goal wasn't to change their own circumstances because they could already work "in a man's world" if that's what they chose to do—they were already entitled, by law, to all the rights and opportunities granted to men.

26

But that wasn't good enough. Their goal was to change the very foundation stones of a society that was already running smoothly—to fundamentally transform the culture to fit their own beliefs—to influence the minds and hearts of others to conform to their ideals. The goal of the Second-Wave feminist was to leave the traditional woman in the dustbin of history and move the female race away from their families and into the more "empowered" and "enlightened" lifestyle of nine-to-five jobs.

Of course, this isn't what feminists will tell you. When you debate a feminist, they will inevitably refer you back to the definition of feminism. So, according to Merriam-Webster, here it is:

# fem·i·nism
*noun* \ˈfe-mə-ˌni-zəm\

": the belief that men and women should have equal rights and opportunities"

Simple as that. Based on the above definition alone, I'd bet 99% of this country is "feminist." That's pretty logical stuff, after all. Of *course* women and men should have equal rights and opportunities. Does *anyone* today—in the year 2014—disagree with that statement, you know, apart from the craziest of the crazy fringe, whom you can't even convince we went to the moon? If this is really the goal of the feminist movement, then congratulations feminists; you've won! *Everyone* is a feminist. You've earned a vacation. Go take a load off and enjoy the fruits of your labor because we now live in a country where we share the same rights and opportunities as men. It's been that way for a while, actually. Seriously, congratulations.

So why is the feminist movement seemingly more loud and outspoken than ever? What injustice is there to fight against now?

This is a classic case of: watch their actions, not their words. Equality was never the goal. The true agenda of the 1960s feminist was nothing more than to blend the genders and legalize abortions. Abortions were the biggest significant legal change for which the Second-Wave Feminist fought. In other words, feminism was birthed simply for the desire to end births. Taking into account the true history of feminism, it's not a correct notion to say that it was built upon the desire for equality. Legal equality already existed. When you get right down to it, feminism was built on the blood of innocent children.

The Silent Genocide

In today's new "Third-Wave Feminism," pro-choice activists have only become louder and bolder, insisting abortion is a "woman's right." They brazenly march the streets, chanting and shouting, and carrying signs with various hand-drawn human anatomy, reading crude and purposely offensive things such as "Not every ejaculation needs a name" and "My uterus > Your God" and "Keep your rosaries off my ovaries." Classy.

Among these strange and disturbing protest signs, there's usually at least one that reads something along the lines of, "Abortion is a Civil Right." This is one of the more baffling and contradictory things about Third-Wave Feminism. Those advocating the ending of millions of innocent lives legitimately see themselves as civil rights warriors. Abortion is not a civil right, but I will give them this: Abortion is a civil rights *issue*. This civil rights issue, however, isn't about the rights of adult women. It's about the rights of the unborn. Every human being has a right to life. This is a right granted to us by God and protected under the Declaration of Independence of the United States. "We hold these truths to be self-evident, that all men are created equal, that they are endowed by their Creator with certain unalienable Rights, that among these are *Life*, Liberty and the pursuit of Happiness." [emphasis added] *Life* is a right. This should be obvious. In fact, the Founders themselves found it so obvious that they called these truths "self-evident." After all, all rights begin with the right to life. Without that basic right to life, all other rights dissolve. But despite logic, it's become almost fashionable for high-profile celebrities to say things like this:

> Can small minded idiot blokes stop telling women whether or not they're entitled to abortions please? #enoughnow… The day the number of single father households equal the number of single mother households is the day I start to listen to their views.
> --Musician, Lily Allan

The last time I checked, I wasn't a "bloke." Neither of the authors of this book are men. In fact, one of us is a *single mother* and we still oppose abortion. Secondly, Lily's suggesting that men aren't entitled to have an opinion on whether or not their children live. Think about the unfairness of that for a minute. Yes, the woman carries the baby, but the baby belongs to the man just as much as it belongs to the woman. Because the father has the potential to love that child just as much as the mother does and the baby could not have existed without him in the first place, he should have an equal say in the matter. Thirdly, Lily's suggesting that it's *men* keeping women from having abortions. This is untrue. It depends on what poll one looks at, but most show about the same percentage of men and women in support of abortion, with women just slightly more in favor than men. But an article from the Guardian paints a different picture:

> [A]round 24 to 35% of men want to put more restrictions on abortion, against 43 to 59% of women – a consistent gap of around 20 percentage points. That raises some pretty big implications, the most obvious being that if it were left to women to vote on the issue, with men out of the picture, there's a good chance that the result would be in favour of restricting abortion. On the flip side, if only men voted, they'd almost certainly vote in favour of women's reproductive rights.

A CBS News/New York Times poll also found that, in 2003, slightly more men believed abortion should be "generally available" than women. If this were really a women's rights issue, shouldn't the vast majority of women be pro-abortion? According to a recent Gallop poll, pro-choice and pro-life women are fairly evenly split down the middle.

Now, I understand why a woman would be pro-abortion because it affects her body personally. But why would a *man* want abortions? One likely reason for this supposed male abortion support might simply be due to fear of being labelled a sexist if they oppose the all-powerful feminist mafia. But what's the deal with those men who actually *do* support abortions? Those men who use their manhood, not to protect innocent lives as true a man should, but to destroy them?

These feminist men are the very picture of misogyny. A man who uses a woman for her body but refuses to commit to her or be held responsible for paying child support if she gets pregnant has everything in the world to gain by the practice of abortions. His sexual pleasure at the expense of countless women may ride on the normalization of such heinous procedures. Many of these supposedly sensitive "pro-choice," "pro-women's reproductive rights" men are in reality selfish, irresponsible boys, the health and wellbeing of women the last thing on their minds. Research shows that 64% of women who had an abortion felt pressured to abort her baby and that pressure often came from her boyfriend or husband. This desire for the normalization of abortions among men is fueled by lust, not love.

I use the term "pro-choice" loosely because it's really only giving one involved party a choice. The other party, the unborn human, has no choice at all in the matter. To claim the living entity inside of a woman's womb is *not* human requires extraordinary denial of, not only moral conscience, but logical and scientific evidence. Especially considering all we know now due to

3D ultrasounds and various other technologies that allow us to observe the baby before birth. We now know that a bright flash of light occurs when the sperm meets the egg, leading some to speculate whether or not this is evidence of the "spirit" entering the child. We know that the heart begins beating at around five weeks, starts moving around on his own at eight weeks, can hiccup at eleven, can feel his mom touch him at twelve, can suck his thumb at fourteen, can sense light at fifteen, kick at sixteen, hear his mother's voice at nineteen… you get the picture. The only difference between a "fetus" and a human adult is *time*. How is it that these abortion supporters can claim it's morally okay to end a human life one second, but the next second, it's murder? Before birth, it's a "health decision" and immediately after, it's something you can earn a life-sentence in prison for? Has anyone asked an abortion supporter when *exactly* a human turns into a human? Because many believe first trimester abortions are fine but second and third are bad. So can they pinpoint the precise minute the "tissue" turns into a baby? The exact *second*? If they were to terminate the pregnancy just after that magic second, does that make it a crime or is there some sort of grace period? And how long is that grace period? I may sound nitpicky here, but if we're talking about potentially *ending human life*, it's only reasonable we should hammer out the details and understand the consequences.

But what if, like President Obama said, I don't want my daughter "punished with a baby" if she makes a mistake?

Having an unwanted pregnancy is totally and one hundred percent avoidable. I'd rather not get into "the talk," but pregnancy doesn't just happen spontaneously. At one point or another, except in cases of rape, you have to make a choice and then you have to live with the consequences of that choice. There are good and bad consequences to every action, some bigger than others. An unplanned pregnancy when one has unprotected sex is one of those possible consequences, just as getting yourself or someone else killed is a possible consequence of driving drunk. It's all about making the right choices. It does nothing but damage ourselves and our kids when we try to take away the consequences of actions. Although, a baby is never a "punishment."

But yes, we all make mistakes. So let's say someone makes a mistake and gets pregnant. Now what? This is why adoption exists. Adoption is a fantastic solution that brings peace to, not only the mother, but another family who possibly couldn't have children of their own. There are thousands of couples out there who would give anything to have the little blessing you are carrying. Isn't turning a mistake into something beautiful better than making a decision that will lead to a lifetime of depression and guilt?

There are countless stories of women who have regretted their abortions. These are things Planned Parenthood and other abortion organizations don't want you to hear. They want you to believe abortions are freeing and healthy, even empowering. A website called Silent No More says otherwise. The site lists pages and pages of testimonies from real women who regret their decision to abort their babies. Here are some heartbreaking excerpts from those testimonies:

My first child was taken from me through the violence of Abortion. This child would never be held, would never be rocked to sleep, would never take his first steps, would never laugh, would never cry, and would never have hopes and dreams in this life because he was not allowed to be born.
--Joan, North Carolina

I don't want to hide my child anymore. He was an innocent causality of a spiritual war...To my precious baby: I will not forget you. I never have. You were always here hidden in my heart. I will not hide you anymore. I love you. To say that I am sorry doesn't seem to be enough.
--Joanne, New York

Having an abortion was one of the hardest things I've ever done...others think that it's time I move on. But I don't think I can, and I don't know if I ever will. All I know is that it hurts.
--Sarah, New Jersey

It still affects me every day of my life, and I wish I could let go of some of this pain. But it has me shackled for the rest of my life.
--Cindy, California

Hurting and still scared, I felt very abandoned and alone because I had no one to talk to about the experience. Those I tried to talk to just laughed at me and pretended like it didn't happen...Years went by living in denial and suppression, and depression and bi-polar conditions took control of my life.
--Sheri, Ohio

I was weeping and screaming, but nothing could turn back time. I felt like a part of me died. I felt angry. I felt guilty. I felt like my world was coming to an end...It was the most beautiful thing I ever created, and I destroyed it.
--Solome, New York

Oh yeah, abortion is *so* healthy, *so* freeing. Tell that to these women. Tell that to the countless women who were also duped or coerced into having abortions. Tell them that they dodged a bullet, that their lives would have been worse if they decided to let the child live. I bet they'd tell you differently.

And tell that to Gianna Jessen, abortion survivor. Planned Parenthood advised Gianna's teenage mother to end the pregnancy when Gianna was seven and a half months old in the womb. However, the saline abortion failed and, by some miracle, Gianna survived. The usual practice at the time for a baby who survived the procedure would have been to end the life by, in Gianna's own words, "strangulation, suffocation, leaving the baby there to die, or throwing the baby away." That didn't happen to her, only because the abortionist wasn't on duty yet and a brave nurse decided to transfer her to a hospital instead, where she was cared for and given to an emergency adoption service.

Unfortunately, Gianna suffered consequences from the actions of her parents and the abortionist. She was born with cerebral palsy as a direct result of the procedure. She now has difficulty walking and has a noticeable limp. However, she'll be the first to tell you she's extraordinarily blessed considering what could've happened that day. Even more incredibly, she's decided to forgive her mother, father, and the abortionist for what they attempted to do and is now using her life to help others and to spread the word about the devastating effects of abortion. She made an excellent point when she said this:

> Today, a baby is a baby when convenient. It is tissue or otherwise when the time is not right. A baby is a *baby* when *miscarriage* takes place at two, three, four months. A baby is called a *tissue* or *clumps of cells* when an *abortion* takes place at two, three, four months. Why is that? I see no difference.
> [emphasis added]

Put yourself in Gianna's shoes for a minute. What if you knew both of your parents, not only wanted you dead, but made an active effort to kill you before you were even born? Imagine them taking you to an organization that is paid millions of dollars every year to murder people exactly like you and then throw you in a garbage can. Most of the time, they successfully exterminate others like you who can't speak or fight back, but imagine you somehow survive, just barely. That, to the professional killers—your very existence—is a "failure."

Gianna's not the only one. There are other women and men out there who survived abortion—some at great cost to their health. These survival cases are becoming rarer as time goes on because science is getting better at aborting successfully. Yay?

Ask yourself honestly: is abortion really good for women? I'm not talking about in the rare cases of rape, incest, or risk to the mother's life. I'm talking about ending a pregnancy out of convenience, like the vast majority of abortions performed in the United States (57,107,921 just since the 70s—five times the number of people killed in the Holocaust). After hearing the stories of those whose lives have been devastated by the tragedy of abortions, it's difficult to see this as "healthy."

Abortion—this silent genocide—is not a women's rights issue. It's a human rights issue. Abortion was made mainstream by people like the racist Margaret Sanger, founder of Planned Parenthood, whose true purpose was to eradicate African Americans. She said this:

> We should hire three or four colored ministers, preferably with social-service backgrounds, and with engaging personalities. The most successful educational approach to the Negro is through a religious appeal. We don't want the word to go out that we want to exterminate the Negro population, and the minister is the man who can straighten out

that idea if it ever occurs to any of their more rebellious members.

Considering black women are *five times* more likely to have an abortion than white women and, though minority women make up only 13% of the female population, minorities constitute *36% of all abortions*, it looks like Margaret's plan is, unfortunately, working according to plan.

It wasn't just African Americans on Margaret's death list, however, but anyone else she deemed unworthy of life. "Birth control must lead ultimately to a cleaner race," she said. Margaret's views led to forced sterilization laws in thirty U.S. states, which resulted in more than 60,000 sterilizations of people considered "feeble-minded," "idiots," or "morons." Yes, this actually happened in America.

Abortion is not about women's rights. It never has been. If it was, Gianna—a *woman*—would have had rights when every adult in her young life made a decision to murder her. Where was the feminist movement for her when she desperately needed protecting? Where were they when she couldn't speak for herself or fight back? No one apart from a single nurse gave her a chance at something as basic as the right to live. But we *all* have it. You, me, and every person reading this was given that chance. Who are we to strip someone else of that right?

## Contradictions as Far as the Eye Can See

To further illustrate the nonsensical nature of feminism, let's look at some of the more common contradictions that are found within the movement. Take, for example, Gloria Steinem, one of the country's most infamous feminists. She said, "A feminist is anyone who recognizes the equality and full humanity of women and men."

And yet...

She's an avid supporter of abortions, even going so far as to flaunt an "I had an abortion" T-shirt to advocate *pride* for the procedure. But abortions, by their very nature, don't recognize the full humanity of all people and definitely don't recognize equality. So, by her own definition, Gloria Steinem is not a feminist.

Then there's this gem from Terry O'Neill, president of the National Organization for Woman (NOW), "From a public health point of view, abortion care, no less than contraception, is an essential measure to prevent the heartbreak of infant mortality..."

Abortions... prevent... infant mortality?

Let that one sink in for a second.

Which reminds us of another conundrum: the birth control issue. We've all been hearing about it non-stop this year—about how evil Hobby Lobby is for not covering birth control for their employees (which, by-the-way is not true. Hobby Lobby covers 16 of the 20 FDA approved forms of birth control. The only four not covered are morning-after or abortion pills, but that's another story). Feminists wail and moan about the injustice of it all—that they can't get free birth control pills from their boss just because they demand it. They boldly proclaim:

*My uterus is none of your business!*

And yet...

They expect Hobby Lobby to *pay* for the decisions they make regarding their uteruses. No one's boss is responsible for one's sex life. That being said, if you work for Hobby Lobby, Hobby Lobby *does* pay for your birth control, yes, even the morning-after pill because, as an employee, you're getting a paycheck from them every two weeks. A paycheck you can use on *whatever* you want, even the morning-after pill if that's what your heart desires. Also, I have great news for you: you're not even required to work for Hobby Lobby. You can get a new job that *does* cover your preferred birth control any time you want, and Hobby Lobby can do absolutely nothing about it. Isn't America great?

Which leads us to another head-scratching declaration by feminists:

*Women are independent and capable human beings who can do anything we put our minds to. We no longer need men to support us!*

And yet...

Feminists show, by their actions, that women are nothing but instinctual animals, totally powerless over their sexual urges, and therefore birth control is absolutely crucial to their very existence. After all, food, water, shelter, and lots of birth control were definitely on Maslow's Hierarchy of Needs, right? Who knows how women survived for millennia without those magic little pills. They must've been some kind of freaks of nature who could control themselves or something. And not only are women incapable of controlling their bodies, but women are also incapable of purchasing said vital birth control on their own, so they need someone else—namely *men*—to pay for it. In other words, to a feminist, women are so strong that they need help with everything.

*Because men are Neanderthals. It's their fault we have un-wanted pregnancies! They only see women as objects to drag around by their hair. As feminists, we need to show them women are intelligent human beings, not mere playthings!*

And yet...

Beyoncé.

Of all the women who turn themselves into sexual objects for money and fame—and, sadly, there are many of them—Beyoncé is one of the most guilty. Take a look at her recent VMA performance (or rather, don't) where she and several other scantily-clad female dancers performed stripteases, gyrated on poles, and sang the words "do you want to touch me, baby?" and "bow down, b*tches" before a massive, cheering audience.

Now, in-and-of-itself, that's not something particularly unheard of on television these days. But what really set the performance apart was, while she actively turned herself into a sexual object for the viewing pleasure of millions of men, the screen behind her boldly portrayed a single, thought-provoking word:

*FEMINIST*

I'll admit it. I'm confused.

Beyoncé's performance, though it's been criticized by some, has been celebrated by many feminists, leading one Huffington Post writer to say Beyoncé is "The Feminist Icon of Our Dreams."

Yes, that I will agree with. Beyoncé is the perfect icon for your cause. Crass? Check. Unladylike? Check. 100% confused about her own beliefs? Check.

*She's just being herself!* feminists say. *That's what feminism is about. Being ourselves, unapologetically, and refusing to change for anyone. Because women are great!*

And yet...

At a very young age, starting in pre-school, feminist society begins to diminish a woman's natural femininity by forcing her into a man's role. They attempt to blend the genders to the point where we don't even know what it means to be a woman anymore, pushing women into careers they may or may not want, forcing them to compete physically with boys in P.E. even though girls' bodies are clearly not built the same, discouraging motherhood and marriage, even going so far as to push for gender neutral bathrooms. They take away everything sacred and unique to women. In other words, women are so much better than men that we need to turn women into... men? And in the same breath, they diminish manhood as well by labeling boys who act like, well, *boys* as disruptive, attention deficit, hyperactive, troublemakers. This only confuses both

45

genders, causing unnecessary stress and repression early on in life. If feminists really believed women are as great as they say, they would stop trying so hard to change them.

*Equal pay for equal work! Close the gender wage gap!*

And yet...

There is no gender wage gap. It's quite simply a myth. "Equal pay" is one of the most dishonest political platforms of our day. It's a lie circulated more than ever due to President Obama's claim that women earn 77 cents to every dollar a man earns. There are countless websites, articles, blogs, and people willing to do basic math that disprove this theory in about two seconds. The Bureau of Labor Statistics report for 2012 seemed to support this myth. But just because a man makes more on average in his lifetime, doesn't mean we have a discrimination problem or a problem at all. The Daily Beast said it best:

> The 23-cent gender pay gap is simply the difference between the average earnings of all men and women working full-time. It does not account for differences in occupations, positions, education, job tenure, or hours worked per week.

In other words, this report pitted a woman who works part-time at Burger King against a man who is a petroleum engineer. This is an apples to oranges comparison. What this report is really saying is that women *choose* to make less money by choosing lower paying jobs. They choose this by placing a higher priority on other things in their lives, like their families, but that doesn't mean there is an injustice. All it means is women are different. Here are some major points to consider when you look at male vs female pay:

1) Women, on average, *choose* careers with lower pay. Of the ten college majors that lead to the most lucrative careers, mainly engineering jobs, men overwhelmingly outnumber women in all but one. And of the ten college majors that lead to the *least* lucrative jobs, things like counseling, the arts, and early childhood education, women overwhelmingly outnumber men in all but one. It's clear much of the supposed "inequality" can be attributed to a woman's personal choice. I'm certain a woman who chose a career in education was very aware she could make more money as a Mechanical Engineer, but she still chose against it. Maybe because working with children made her, oh, I don't know, happy? What a wacky concept.

2) "Men [are] almost twice as likely as women to work more than 40 hours a week, and women almost twice as likely to work only 35 to 39 hours per week." Women, on average, miss more work than men *even when they don't have children*. There are a lot of factors that go into this, including the fact that women's bodies work differently, causing different health issues and limitations. It was reported that women call in sick about 189 times in a lifetime while men call in about 140 times.

3) Lastly, yes, women also have children. Therefore, naturally, they take more time off from work, be it for maternity leave, child care when they can't find a babysitter, taking care of sick kids, and so on. This leads to women working fewer hours on average than men and, as a result, leads to a woman making less money *in her lifetime*. But that has absolutely nothing to do with pay rate and salary.

*That's not fair! Women shouldn't be punished economically just because it's in their biological natures to give birth to children!*

This is an argument common among proponents of "equal pay." But who exactly is to blame for this? God Himself? And how do you propose we solve this supposed pay inequality? Would we pay women for just as many hours as men, even when they didn't work those hours? I have to say, that'd be pretty nice. Until you actually think about the ramifications.

Let's say a woman chooses to take a year off to spend time with her brand new baby. Who's going to pay her salary for that year? The company? The company isn't going to appreciate having to pay someone for all that time when they're not working. They likely couldn't afford to do so, even if they wanted to. And if the company was required to do this for *all* their female employees, wouldn't it make more financial sense to hire male workers instead? It'd be much cheaper for them in the long run to hire men who don't have to take maternity leave and don't have debilitating cramps every month. So, if the company was required to make up this difference in pay, it could actually *cause* discrimination, putting more women out of work as they're replaced by their male counterparts. This would damage working women more than any imaginary wage gap ever could.

Ultimately, when you take into account all of these factors, when you look at an individual woman and an individual man working the same job for the same number of hours, this massive 23-cent-gap, on average, shrinks all the way down to a miniscule…

Five cents.

Yes, the *actual* gender wage gap is only five cents. Still, it's not fair, but it's not nearly as dire as feminists would have you believe. There are questions as to why this small difference still exists. Many attribute it to a small degree of fringe discrimination or the fact that men are more assertive and are more willing to ask for a raise than women. I will tell you this though: between both of the women writing this book, we have a combined job history in areas such as retail, hospitality, customer service, cosmetology, sales, data entry, dictation for the hearing impaired, and quality assurance. Never once has either of us, or any woman we know, ever had a lower rate of pay than a male doing the same work. To assume the average employer would be sexist enough to even attempt that is insanity. The gender wage gap is nothing more than a lie perpetrated by politicians as a means to manipulate voters. Just like Edward Bernays' successful attempt at convincing women to smoke, this modern-day manipulation seems to be working out nicely.

But I digress. It's true; it's not fair that women have to take more time off from work than men. However, the fault doesn't belong to anyone or anything except basic human biology. No one, be it an employer or a tax payer, should be required to make up for biology's disparity. Passing on the burden doesn't get rid of the burden. Maybe we're looking at this from the wrong angle completely. Maybe the fact that women miss more work goes to show that, by our very natures, we're not meant to be breadwinners in the first place.

*Okay, but women should have the right to choose!* shout the feminists. *Every woman is different and they should be able to live their lives however they see fit!*

And yet...
Feminists say things like this:

No woman should be authorized to stay at home and raise her children. Society should be totally different. Women should not have that choice, precisely because if there is such a choice, too many women will make that one.
--Simone de Beauvoir

This quote is an interesting one. The woman who said it was a radical, but I'd be willing to bet a lot of modern-day feminists still have her way of thinking, even if it's not said aloud. This quote alone proves feminism is a lie. It's a way of controlling women and forcing them to be whatever men and other, more bitter, women want them to be. If feminism was really about empowering women, then why take away their choices? If having a career outside the home really is the ideal lifestyle, then why does she admit "too many women" would make the decision to stay home? Obviously, not all women are alike, but I contend the majority of women would want to stay home if they were at all to do so because that's the role that generally comes more naturally to women. *That's* what women find empowering. If feminism really is for the benefit of women, we should encourage all women to make the decision that's right for them on an *individual* basis and not demean them when we think they are making the "wrong" choices.

*You know what would solve the problem? If men would join hands with us! It would be wonderful to see more male feminists in the world—men who can finally empathize with our oppression.*

And yet...

When a man *does* empathize in the most extreme way possible—to actually attempt to *become* a woman by means of surgery or cosmetic alterations, the radical, all-inclusive, "loving left" feminists refuse to let him enter the fold.

A recent article from The New Yorker entitled "What Is a Woman?" explained that, on the one hand, transgender women often believe they were born with a woman's brain inside a man's body. On the other hand, radical feminists believe there's no such thing as a "male" or "female" brain—that our differences are purely the imprints of society and culture. These same feminists suggest that transgender women still experience "male privilege" and, therefore, shouldn't be allowed to call themselves women. In 1973, Robin Morgan said this:

> I will not call a male "she"; thirty-two years of suffering in this androcentric society, and of surviving, have earned me the title "woman"; one walk down the street by a male transvestite, five minutes of his being hassled (which he may enjoy), and then he dares, he *dares* to think he understands our pain? No, in our mothers' names and in our own, we must not call him sister.

Many radical feminists still believe that notion. The same article from The New Yorker explains those feminists' position:

> Anyone born a man retains male privilege in society; even if he chooses to live as a woman — and accept a correspondingly subordinate social position — the fact that he has a choice means that he can never understand what being a woman is really like. By extension, when trans women demand to

be accepted as women they are simply exercising another form of male entitlement.

On the flip side, transgender women will tell you they have no such "choice"—that their behavior and dress is a result of a physical discrepancy between their brains and bodies—that they were born that way. This is a belief that sparked a recent protest at a "RadFem Responds" rally. Transgender activists responded with "acts of vandalism — stealing electrical cables, cutting water pipes, keying cars in the parking lot, and spray-painting a six-foot penis, and the words 'Real Women Have D–ks,' on the side of the main kitchen tent."

When both sides of the argument make absolutely no sense, you know the world has been turned completely upside-down. It seems even feminism doesn't know what feminism stands for.

Was the feminist movement ever really necessary? Maybe at one point it was. Maybe at one time it wasn't a hateful, divisive movement that imagines up fake injustices and silences common sense. Either way, the hard reality is the feminism of today is not loving, not inclusive, and does not stand for the rights of women.

# FEMINIST FAIRY TALE

## THE PRINCESS WHO DIDN'T NEED NO MAN

ONCE upon a time there was a ~~beautiful princess~~ strong, independent woman who was born to a ~~king and queen~~ single mother. Her mother and father were never married. In fact, she never knew her father because he left before she was even born. That wasn't a problem though because her mother was also a strong, independent woman who didn't need a man's help raising her little independent woman.

So the little, strong, independent woman grew into her teenage years and started high school where she fell in ~~love~~ lust with ~~a handsome prince~~ some guy.

Now, this woman was more than just strong and independent, she was also intelligent. She kept up with all the most popular TV shows and rap music, so she knew that marriage was archaic. A strong, independent woman such as herself, didn't need to be tied down to just one man. Sleeping around isn't just okay, it's liberating. Gloria Steinem told her so.

That's why she couldn't predict how heartbroken she'd be once she had sex with the guy, and he left her for another girl. Sex is a harmless past time after all, so why was she distraught?

The guy didn't just leave her with heartbreak, he also left her with a baby, and because of this, she had to drop out of high school.

So the strong, independent woman moved into a ~~castle~~ one-bedroom apartment downtown and got a minimum wage job to support her and her son. But it was okay because if anyone could do it on her own, it was *this* independent woman. However, she didn't make enough money at her job to survive, so she called on ~~her fairy godmother~~ the government to supply her with fancy, new ~~glass slippers~~ food stamps.

Still, she longed for a male companion, not only for the financial stability but also to fill emotional needs. This made no sense to her. She was always taught she didn't need a man. Yet, something inside her yearned for someone to fill that gap in her heart, the gap left by her own father so many years ago. She went from man to man, searching for someone to make her whole. In her desperation, this strong, independent woman gave too much of herself and fell into the arms of abusers.

Years passed. She worked hard at miserable, entry level jobs and became bitter about missing out on precious moments with her son. She drowned her sorrows in alcohol, prescription medication, illegal drugs—whatever was around.

This strong, independent woman's son grew up. He went on to be an upstanding young criminal and a frequent visitor to the state penitentiary for imitating the only father figures he'd ever known. The strong, independent woman, still living in poverty, had emotional scars so deep they never healed.

~~And they lived happily ever after~~.

# 4

## THE WAR ON MARRIAGE

WE have to abolish and reform the institution of marriage. . . . By the year 2000 we will, I hope, raise our children to believe in human potential, not God. . . . We must understand what we are attempting is a revolution, not a public relations movement.

--Gloria Steinem

A liberated woman is one who has sex before marriage and a job after.

--Gloria Steinem

The complete destruction of traditional marriage and the nuclear family is the 'revolutionary or utopian' goal of feminism.

--Kate Millett

We can't destroy the inequities between men and women until we destroy marriage.
--Robin Morgan

Since marriage constitutes slavery for women, it is clear that the women's movement must concentrate on attacking this institution. Freedom for women cannot be won without the abolition of marriage.
--Sheila Cronin

Marriage as an institution developed from rape as a practice.
--Andrea Dworkin

Marriage has existed for the benefit of men; and has been a legally sanctioned method of control over women.... We must work to destroy it. The end of the institution of marriage is a necessary condition for the liberation of women. Therefore it is important for us to encourage women to leave their husbands and not to live individually with men.... All of history must be re-written in terms of oppression of women. We must go back to ancient female religions like witchcraft.
--"The Declaration of Feminism," 1971

It's clear that a lot of feminists have, um, *negative* views on marriage. This hatred for marriage has been a running theme among the radical variety for decades. I suspect women such as those listed above have deep emotional scarring from some painful events in their lifetimes, so getting a feminist like this to view marriage in a healthy light is near-impossible. But what about the non-radical, everyday feminist who is fine with marriage? (By-the-way, rhetorical question to those feminists: are you okay with the people above representing your cause? Because, yeesh, I'd vote them off the island.)

I contend that feminism ruins marriages.

*What? How can that be? Feminism saves marriages!*

Thank you for that, feminist book critic who speaks only in italics. Before we get into how feminism hurts marriages, let's first counter the ridiculous notions of the above radical feminists and look at how marriage benefits us all. A good marriage is *good* for you. I mean *really* good for you, and in practically every way. According to FamilyFacts.org, here are just some of the most obvious benefits of being married:

- "Married couples report greater sexual satisfaction."

- "Married women report higher levels of physical and psychological health."
- "Married people are more likely to volunteer."
- "Being married increases the likelihood of affluence."
- "Married people tend to experience less depression and fewer problems with alcohol."
- "Getting married increases the probability of moving out of a poor neighborhood."
- "Married men make more money."
- "Ever-married women are less likely to experience poverty."
- "Marriage is associated with a lower mortality risk."

Make that a *much* lower mortality risk. An eight-year-long study was performed by UCLA and they found that single men, who were in good health, were 88% more likely to die throughout the course of the study than those who were married. *Eighty-eight percent!* My gosh, single men. Get married immediately. Your life may depend on it.

Based on those statistics, I think it's pretty clear that we should all get married. And we shouldn't just get married. If at all possible, we should get married *young.*

*Get married young? Are you crazy? Studies have shown people who marry young have much higher divorce rates than those who marry later in life.*

You may be referring to the study done by the National Survey of Family Growth which concluded those who marry before 25 have a 50% higher divorce rate than those who marry older. One problem with this study is that they group married couples who are 24 with those who get married in their teen years. The maturity gap between a 16-year-old and a 24-year-old is massive, therefore it isn't exactly fair to group them all together statistically.

Several other factors contribute to divorce rates, besides age including: level of education, race, religion, income, family background, etc. One very important piece to the puzzle is whether or not the couple cohabitated before marriage. Cohabitation prior to marriage increases risk of divorce significantly. Financial stresses are often a big factor in divorce as well, and since most teenagers and 20-somethings aren't exactly rolling in the dough, especially in this age of widespread unemployment and massive student loan debt, it's only natural there would be a higher level of divorce among the young. But this has little to do with the age of the couple and more to do with external circumstances that would strain even the most mature of relationships. The

Census Bureau in 1993 found that married couples who lived in poverty were far more likely to divorce, regardless of age.

Perhaps the most important risk factor is whether or not the couple had other sexual partners before marriage. If they did, this also increases the risk of divorce—the more partners one has before marriage, the higher the risk. In fact, the divorce rate for couples who remained completely abstinent before marriage is only *five percent*. Read that last sentence again. Based on this fact, the most important thing you can do to prepare for a lasting marriage, regardless of age, is to remain abstinent. Knowing that remaining abstinent becomes less likely as one gets older, it's only logical to conclude that getting married young can actually *reduce* risk of divorce, but only if the couple hasn't slept together first.

In fact, research done by the National Center for Biotechnology Information concluded that, in terms of longitude and happiness levels, the best time to marry is between the ages of 22-25, ages that are considered young by the current national standards. The quality of marriage was shown to decrease if the couple married at the age of 26 and beyond.

Individuals have been getting married very young for millennia and even in fairly recent decades. Take a look at the chart below, for example, reflecting the U.S. Census Bureau statistics on median married age. The top line reflects the male age and the bottom reflects the female age.

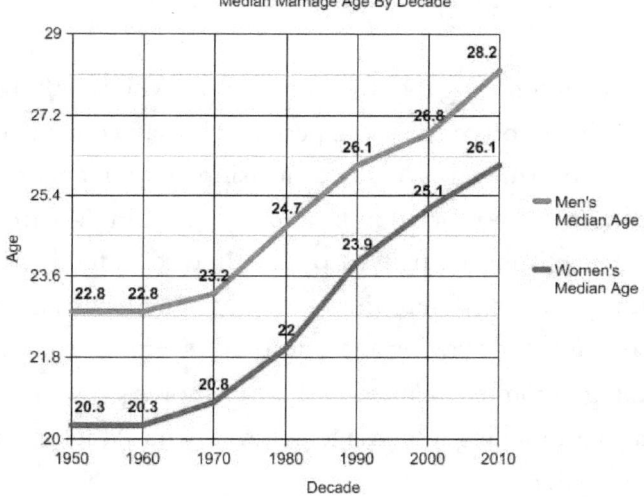

Median Marriage Age By Decade

As you can see, 20 and 22 were the median ages that women and men got married, respectively, in the 1950s. That has jumped to 26 and 28 in the modern day. As most of us know, the divorce rate has become steadily worse over the course of these decades. Of course, correlation does not always equal causation, but it's unwise to turn a blind eye to correlation entirely. Another correlation to consider is that from the 1960s until now, the ideology of feminism has been on the rise along with the rise of divorce rates.

*But young people are so… young. They don't know what they want for breakfast, let alone what they want in a spouse! They need more life experience before they settle down.*

It's interesting that the same people who say things like this are often the same people who say young people *can* be trusted to make a decision as permanent as getting a tattoo, or as important as choosing a career path or putting their lives on the line to defend their country, or as life-altering as having gender reassignment surgery or having an abortion. It seems to me that making a commitment to end a life should be a bigger deal than making a marriage commitment. At least one is reversible.

The notion that single people need to have more life experience before marriage is a damaging mindset. Recently, I came across a comment on Facebook by a friend of a friend, trying to convince a young woman she needed to wait several more years to get married because she hadn't "travelled enough yet."

It's painfully obvious people like this don't understand marriage at all. It's emotionally dangerous to think of marriage as an end goal rather than a beginning. If everyone waited until they were financially settled, completed all their education, and had done everything they wanted to do in life *before* they got married, our marriage rates would be almost nonexistent. At the risk of sounding like a cheesy Facebook meme: marriage is a journey, not a destination. It's about experiencing life and growing *together*. Waiting to get married later in life can present a whole new set of problems precisely *because* most people in their 30s, 40s, 50s *do* have more of life figured out. Their personalities are mostly set in stone, unlike twenty-somethings who are still developing. A young person who's still developing can more easily adapt to another person, just like a young child has an easier time learning a new language. The older one gets, the more accustomed one becomes to living a certain way and the harder it is to allow someone into that life. Not to mention, the older one becomes, the more emotional, financial, and romantic baggage one carries with them into the marriage. It's an unfortunate fact of life that more life brings more baggage. Marrying younger prevents much of these problems.

Not only is the argument to marry older detrimental to marriages, it's also detrimental to birth rates.

*Well, good!* the average feminist would say. *We're overpopulated as it is. We need fewer babies on the earth.*

I could write an entire book on why this particular argument is not true. Instead, I'm going to humbly ask you to check out this website full of fun videos that will hold your attention much better than I could and will, hopefully, put your mind at ease about so-called over-population. It's called overpopulationisamyth.com. The website goes into detail as to why we sometimes *feel* overpopulated, namely in large cities where we willingly crowd together, when in actuality, most of the world is just empty space. It also illustrates, among other things, that we have plenty of food on the planet to feed everyone, that a higher population *decreases* poverty, and that every family currently living in the *entire world* could have a house and a yard and live comfortably in an area the size of Texas. Any problems we have with feeding the world stem from corrupt politics and greed, not lack of resources.

I will also add that having lots of babies is *good* for us economically speaking. The problem is, in a poor economy, like the one we're experiencing now, people tend to have fewer children due to lack of finances. However, economists have proven this mindset actually hurts the economy as a whole. A CBS News article explains:

> We tend to think economic growth comes from working harder and smarter. But economists attribute up to a third of it to more people joining the workforce each year than leaving it.

Because we had the lowest birth rates in recorded history in 2012, this is concerning. Not only do we need new people to enter the workforce consistently for the sake of growing the economy, but we need them to enter the workforce just to support future Social Security and Medicare programs. Currently, three full-time workers are required to support one Social Security recipient and we need almost three full-time workers for every Medicare recipient as well. These programs were designed for a society that is growing or, at the very least, remaining the same. In order to maintain our current population, every woman in the United States would need to have an average of 2.1 children—one to replace her, one to replace him, and maybe a third to make up for those who die young. And those numbers would only keep our population the same assuming there were no wars, famine, natural disasters, or fatal disease to counteract it. In reality, every fertile woman needs to have *more* than two kids each simply to maintain our population and in order to make up for those who are infertile or choose not to have kids. But this is not happening. We're not keeping up with the birthrate required to keep us at our current population.

Other countries, like Japan, are much worse off than the Western World. Japan actually had more deaths than births in 2012. It's reported their population is shrinking by one citizen every one hundred seconds and, if they are to continue at this rate, their entire population would be extinct in just 1,000 years.

But I digress to the issue at hand: feminism and marriage. How does just a little bit of everyday feminism ruin a healthy marriage? Apart from the office romances that stem from having more women in the workforce, which harm relationships (more on that later), feminism also confuses gender roles at home and, therefore, confuses marriages. Even a seemingly harmless thing like household chores can present a huge problem.

A Norwegian study entitled "Equality in the Home" found that husbands and wives who share household work had a 50% higher divorce rate than those where the woman shouldered most of it. "Maybe it's sometimes seen as a good thing to have very clear roles with lots of clarity," said Thomas Hansen, co-author of the study, "...where one person is not stepping on the other's toes."

(By-the-way, their research also found the women who did most of the housework were reported to be just as happy as the women who shared the work.)

But the toe-stepping doesn't end with chores. A man is naturally inclined to be the breadwinner, so if a woman invades that territory, it creates competition. Suddenly, instead of focusing on a happy marriage, both parties are comparing relative incomes, spending habits, and responsibilities, keeping an imaginary score-card in their heads that will inevitably spill out during their next argument.

And the man is *always* going to lose this argument. Researchers found that even when women work out-side the home, they still shoulder about three times as much housework as their husbands. Who wants to be responsible for *all* the work? Quite honestly, if a man required me to do all the housework *and* work outside the home, I wouldn't be a happy camper. But it isn't always the husband's fault. This is simply the fruits of feminism. Just as men are naturally inclined to be breadwinners, women are naturally inclined to take care of the home front. It's nearly impossible for women to let go of their innate responsibilities simply because they're taking on others. It's a natural female impulse for a woman to want to take care of the "nest," no mat-ter how tired she is and no matter how many other re-sponsibilities she's taken on. Unfortunately, it's not possible to do everything without letting one area slip, having a nervous breakdown, or both. And when she does have that breakdown, she will blame her husband.

This brings to mind that hilariously unrealistic En-joli perfume ad from the 80s called "The 24 Hour Woman" that taught us the ultimate woman can "bring home the bacon" (have a career) and "fry it up in the pan" (cook) "and never let you forget you're a man." It goes on to say, "I can work 'til five o'clock, come home and read Tickety-Tock, and if it's lovin' you want, I can kiss you and give you the shivers."

Hmm. A woman who cooks, makes money, *and* still has the time and energy for sex. Sounds like an ad written by a man to me. Remember our talk about propaganda manipulating the minds of feminists? Perhaps something to think about.

# Feminist Fairy Tale

## The Useless Prince and the Strong Independent Maiden

ONCE upon a time, there was a ~~handsome prince~~ useless man who was ~~dashing and chivalrous~~ completely unnecessary.

One beautiful morning the useless man was busy ~~slaying a dragon~~ doing something I'm sure a woman could do better, when he heard the cry of a ~~fair maiden~~ strong, independent woman coming from the Enchanted Forest.

So the useless man finished up his cute little work and ran to save the woman. Her screams led him to a tall tower in the center of the forest.

"Strong, independent woman!" he cried to the top of the tower. "Let down your hair so that I may climb up and rescue you!"

"*Excuse me?*" the woman replied. "What makes you think I need rescuing?"

"But I—weren't you... screaming in terror?"

"Well, yeah, because I'm in danger."

"Then please, dear maid—uh, strong woman—let me rescue you!"

"Pfft, why? So you can use me for my body? So you can subjugate me and walk all over me? No thank you."

"Nay! So that you may no longer be in peril!"

"Boy, you're arrogant, aren't you? Swooping in here, deciding I need help, and then suggesting I need *you* to save me? This is the fifteenth century! I'm a strong, independent woman who don't need no man."

The ~~prince~~ useless man sighed. "I didn't—I wasn't suggesting—Look, I'm just trying to do the right thing—"

"Puh-*leez*! I don't need your help, *man*. Now run along and do whatever it is you useless men do. Besides, I cut off all my hair."

"Wha—*why?*"

"Because I wasn't going to be defined by my femininity. I'm not merely an object of your pleasure!"

The man threw his hands in the air. "I never thought you were!"

"And let's say I *do* let you 'rescue' me, though the concept is laughable for men are useless, what happens then? You force me to marry you in exchange?"

"No! Of course not—"

"And I become your personal servant for the rest of my life?"

"Well, no. You'd live in a glorious castle and be an equal partner in ruling our kingdom."

"Aha! So you *do* want to marry me, you chauvinist swine."

The man sat against the base of the tower wall and sighed at the sky. "I beg of you, let me save you so that I may go my way and pray I never have the misfortune of crossing paths with you again."

"No."

"Fine," The man stood. "I hope you and your tower will be very miserable together!"

The woman let out a humorless laugh. "See! This is exactly what I'm talking about. Chivalry is dead."

The man walked away feeling frustrated and confused and the woman died alone in her tower.

~~And they lived happily ever after.~~

# 5

## THE WAR ON MEN

FOR the past few years, the illusive idea of a "War on Women" has been spouted by the media, politicians, and activists, trying their best to turn the entire female gender into a group of victims. They've got it backwards. There *is* a War on Women, but it's being perpetrated by the very people pointing the fingers—by those who actively set out to squash femininity and prevent women from being the best *women* (not men) we can be. To open our eyes to the true War on Women, we need only look at a couple of the demeaning attacks on housewives and mothers that have been circulated by feminists.

> Being a housewife is an illegitimate profession... The choice to serve and be protected and plan towards being a family-maker is a choice that shouldn't be. The heart of radical feminism is to change that.
> --Vivian Gornick

...[B]eing a mother isn't really work. Yes, of course, it's something—actually, it's something almost every woman at some time does, some brilliantly and some brutishly and most in the boring middle of making okay meals and decent kid conversation. But let's face it: It is not a selective position.
--Elizabeth Wurtzel

[Housewives] are dependent creatures who are still children... parasites.
--Gloria Steinem

A parasite sucking out the living strength of another organism...the [housewife's] labor does not even tend toward the creation of anything durable. [W]oman's work within the home [is] not directly useful to society, produces nothing. [The housewife] is subordinate, secondary, parasitic.
--Simone de Beauvoir

Feminists love to preach about how all women should have the choice to do what they want but then judge and degrade those who don't choose *their* way. It's perplexing that most feminists will say careers in areas such as childcare, education, and the culinary arts are worthy goals for women, however, to use those same talents—nurturing children, teaching children, and cooking—in a woman's own home is somehow less noble, or even reprehensible. There is no difference between the two paths except the former has external rewards and the latter has internal rewards. In other words, feminists have diminished a talented and skillful woman into nothing—a near-worthless human being—if no dollar amount is placed on her head. The feminist movement seeks only to praise women who pursue money and power as opposed to women who pursue things of more lasting value.

If you'll notice, all of the assaults above came from, not men, but women—women attacking other women. If a real "war on women" exists, this is it.

But that's another story. What I want to talk about is the rarely mentioned War on *Men*.

*War on Men? Well, that's just nutty!*

At the risk of driving you to repeatedly smash your book against the wall, I'm going to make you read more quotes from feminists. I'm sorry.

> The male is a domestic animal which, if treated with firmness... can be trained to do most things.
> --Jilly Cooper

Men are rapists, batterers, plunderers, killers; these same men are religious prophets, poets, heroes, figures of romance, adventure, accomplishment, figures ennobled by tragedy and defeat. Men have claimed the earth, called it 'Her.' Men ruin Her. Men have airplanes, guns, bombs, poisonous gases, weapons so perverse and deadly that they defy any authentically human imagination.

--Andrea Dworkin

I feel that 'man-hating' is an honourable and viable political act, that the oppressed have a right to class-hatred against the class that is oppressing them.

--Robin Morgan

As long as some men use physical force to subjugate females, all men need not. The knowledge that some men do suffices to threaten all women. He can beat or kill the woman he claims to love; he can rape women... he can sexually molest his daughters... *the vast majority of men in the world do one or more of the above.*

--Marilyn French

> The proportion of men must be reduced to and maintained at approximately 10% of the human race.
>
> --Sally Miller Gearhart

Gee, tell us how you *really* feel, girls.

Imagine for a minute that these quotes were reversed—that they were being said by men about *women* instead. Imagine if a male activist declared that all women were terrible human beings and the female race needed to be reduced to only ten percent of the world's population. Can you imagine the outcry? We'd never hear the end of it. The man who said these horrific things would be publically shamed, called all sorts of names, and maybe even fired from his job. But because these were said by women and against men, most of us probably haven't even heard these quotes before. The double standard is undeniable. And this is just the tip of the iceberg when it comes to feminist man-hating.

In today's society, men aren't allowed to complain about sexism because that somehow makes *them* sexist or misogynistic or politically incorrect. That's ridiculous and unfair, considering *all* gender issues affect *both* genders. So allow me—a woman—to complain for them.

Men and women are undeniably and deeply connected. One can't damage one without damaging the other. Unfortunately for everyone, society is awful to

81

our men today. On the one hand, we've torn them away from their natural strengths and forced their role onto women, but on the other hand, we berate them and call them "lazy" or "useless" for doing exactly what society has told them to do, which is share the work. When they compete with women, the way feminist society claims they want, they're seen as brutes, but if they go easy on women, they're sexist. Feminists tell them they should decline to open doors and pay for dinner because being a gentleman is somehow offensive, but on the other hand, we scold them for being un-chivalrous. I can't imagine how confusing this must be.

Speaking to the ladies in particular for a second, have you ever stopped to think about this? About how hard it must be to lose out on a job you're fully qualified for, simply because Affirmative Action requires the company to hire a woman instead? To have fewer education opportunities than women because there are *four times* more scholarships specifically for women than men? (Perhaps this is one reason more women than men have been attending college since the 1970s.) To constantly be blamed for every ill regarding the family; to always be the bad guy in every relationship; to have your entire identity warped and confused and, on top of that, never being allowed to mention the injustice of it all?

This isn't even taking into account how unfairly boys are treated in the American public school system. As Christina Hoff Sommers from the American Enterprise Institute explained, boys are five times more likely than girls to be expelled from preschool (*preschool*. What heinous act could a four-year-old do that would warrant expulsion, I wonder). In the following grades, all the way through their senior year of high school, boys account for about 70% of all suspensions. These suspensions are many times for innocent, boy-like behavior (for instance, a seven-year-old Maryland boy named Josh Welch was recently sent home from school for biting a Pop Tart into the shape of a gun). Boys generally receive lower grades, win fewer honors, and as mentioned, are less likely to go to college. An institute called Third Way found in their research that boys are less organized, less attentive, perform worse socially than girls, and boys are less likely to ask a question on a subject they don't understand. The study reads:

> The social and behavioral skills gap between boys and girls is considerably larger than the gap between children from poor families and middle class families or the gap between black and white children.

This gap is not evidence of boys being academically inferior to girls, rather this is evidence of an extreme bias in favor of the way girls learn. For example, when it comes to creative writing in the classroom, educators often favor emotional personal narratives, something writer instructor Ralph Fletcher calls the "Confessional Poet" style of writing. But that's the preferred writing style of girls, not boys. Boys tend to enjoy writing about more action-centered stories involving heroes and villains. These stories aren't valued in the same way by those handing out the grades. This causes their grades to suffer, which often results in lower self-esteem. Psychologist Michael Thompson summed it up this way, "If you treat girls as the gold standards and boys as defective girls, that's going to be demoralizing. What do elementary and junior high girls always say about boys their age? 'You are so immature.' If that's the norm, then this system is just rigged against the boys."

And the amount of recess time, something young boys need in order to work off their excess energy, has been severely cut back in recent years. This causes boys to be more hyperactive during class. This in turn causes more behavioral problems, which will inevitably get him punished or forced on drugs like Ritalin or Adderall to "normalize" him. This is a hyperactivity many boys will grow out of naturally. Nearly 20% of all American boys are diagnosed with ADHD and many of those diagnoses are simply because the boy is acting too much like a boy. Ryan D'Agostino wrote an informative piece for Esquire.com on the effects this has on the American boy. These drugs contain many harmful side effects, including the severe risk of dependency, leading Adderall to be the most commonly abused drug among high school seniors. These drugs can cause bipolar tendencies, aggressive behavior, weight loss, sleeping trouble, glazed over eyes, paranoid feelings, facial tics, sudden death for children with heart conditions, even thoughts of suicide. The only diagnostic method to determine whether or not a boy will be prescribed Ritalin or Adderall is a simple questionnaire and a short conversation with a doctor. These medications may be necessary for some who truly have a disorder, but if one in five boys really need this kind of mind-altering drug just to survive the American school system, this is clear evidence that schools need to better accommodate a boy's method of learning. Boys become men and men are wildly important to the healthy function of a community. Crippling them with thoughts of inadequacy so early in their lives is crippling to the world as well.

With a society so intent on shaming the masculinity out of boys and men, it's no wonder terms like "toxic masculinity" have become so common. "Toxic masculinity" has been used to describe behaviors such as sexual harassment and assault, disrespect towards women or minorities, arrogance, overly aggressive behavior, and even rape. The term implies that an excess of masculinity causes these egotistical, antagonistic, and violent behaviors. But is this fair? If toxic masculinity exists, then logic dictates the converse, "toxic femininity," must exist as well. But we never hear of such a thing. Imagine for a moment what the toxic version of femininity would look like. It's difficult to think of many "toxic feminine traits." To say there is such a thing is to assume there are women out there who are too female and must repress their femininity for the good of society. How anti-woman would *that* be?

The feminists, however, are teaching young men just that. They're essentially telling a man that being too much of a man is toxic to those around him. But he *is* a man. So, what is their solution? Be less of himself? We live in a society that emboldens absolutely everyone to "be true to themselves," "don't change for anyone," "you were born this way," and "you do you," unless... you're a man. If you're a man, you must suppress your natural state for the good of the collective. According to feminists, men must be more like women because there's something inherently wrong with men. But this is a dangerous mindset. Masculinity is not the cause of violence and rape, and it's outrageously offensive to assume such. In fact, boys who grow up *without* father figures—*without enough masculine influence in their lives*—are far more likely to become violent and aggressive. If any-thing, it's a *lack* of masculinity that causes these negative behaviors. True masculinity is defensive not offensive, and it's been traditionally viewed as such. Masculinity is absolutely crucial to *prevent* violence towards others.

But despite the feminists' claim that they're out to protect women, the feminist-dominated media is de-termined to smother this protective influence, or at the very least, ridicule it to death. How many TV shows, movies, or books have you seen recently where the pro-tagonist is a strong, attractive, or sophisticated female who can do no wrong, meanwhile a ridiculous, idiotic man screws everything up? This blatant propaganda becomes even more obvious when we look at TV show fathers in particular. In the past, the typical TV father was the wise, responsible, benevolent patriarch who gave sage advice and, though stern, loved his family un-conditionally; the *Leave It to Beaver*, *Father Knows Best* trend of the 1950s. But since the rise of feminism, a shift so dramatic has occurred that it's broken the pen-dulum entirely, stomped it to death, and thrown it into the incinerator. Today, the "Bumbling Dad" TV trope is what we've come to expect. Tvtropes.org says this:

Born out of the Sitcom Dysfunctional Family, he's a deliberate subversion of the Standard '50s Father.

Now so ubiquitous the older trope is nearly forgotten.

Although he's clever at times, he's not usually allowed to be smart. He has no idea that shortcuts make long delays. He's lazy, gluttonous and has miscellaneous other glaring vices. His children may love him, but they often don't respect him. However, he is still a sympathetic character; the source of his charm is his complete love and loyalty to his family, even if the main way he shows it is by fixing problems he caused himself.

His family is made up of at least one child nearing or in their teenage years, and a wife (usually much prettier than Dad) who spends her time parenting the husband.

Homer Simpson may be the most obvious example of this mockery of fatherhood, but this stereotype has shown up to some degree in almost every modern sitcom. Frank Barone from *Everybody Loves Raymond*, Tim Taylor from *Home Improvement*, Al Bundy from *Married... with Children*, Hal from *Malcolm in the Middle*, Herman Munster from *The Munsters*, Walter Nichols from *Drake & Josh*, Earl Sinclair from *Dinosaurs*, Peter Griffin from *Family Guy*, and Phil Dunphy from *Modern Family* are just a few examples. The list goes on in movies, video games, books, and advertisements. And it's not just fathers; it's men in general. If there's a character who is weak-minded, constantly messing everything up, or just plain stupid, it's most likely a male character. These may be humorous characters, and the writers of them may have had no other intention but to entertain, but this has become a problem. Almost nothing is as influential to our minds as the entertainment we consume. Are these the models of fatherhood our boys have to look up to? With this kind of mainstream propaganda, is it any wonder our society looks down on men? Is it any wonder in recent years sexist terms like "mansplain" (meaning condescendingly explaining something to a woman, usually in a clueless and overconfident manner) have been added to the collective vocabulary? Again, think about this honestly: if the roles of these fictitious characters were reversed, do you think anyone would stand for it? Most likely, there would be widespread outrage, and most of these shows would be boycotted out of existence. Because women are divine goddesses who can do anything twice as well as a man… right?

Not Exactly. Women aren't perfect. Women *can't* do everything a man can do, and that's by design. How many women (apart from those terrifying body builder types) can successfully beat the average man in a contest of physical strength? How many women can just *will* themselves pregnant without the help of a man? How many children can grow up without a father figure and honestly say it hasn't deeply scarred and emotionally handicapped them? How many women can effectively suppress their hormones every month, including those irrational meltdowns, and keep a level head as successfully as a man? Let's face it; guys are generally better assets in stressful situations and research proves it. Women are more than twice as likely to develop anxiety disorders. An article entitled "Are Women Wired to Worry?" on Promises.com said this:

> This is a controversial idea and one that many people are reluctant to talk about for fear of appearing sexist. There may be some truth to it, though. In 1990, researchers discovered a brain signal that they called the ERN, or error-related negativity signal. This is an electrical wave in the brain, which can be seen on brain scans, produced when a person makes a mistake while trying to complete some type of task. People who worry more create a bigger ERN.
>
> In one study regarding the ERN, researchers scanned the brains of both male and female participants while they took a simple test. The study subjects also completed the "Penn State Worry Questionnaire," a survey that is commonly used by professionals to assess a person's level of anxiety. The results of the study showed that women who

scored higher on the questionnaire, those with more anxiety, had much bigger ERN signals after making mistakes on the test.

The questionnaire indicated several male participants were also big worriers, but they did not show the same big ERN signals that the high-anxiety women did. As the tasks on the test became more difficult, the anxious women made more mistakes and created more ERN signals. Women seem to have a more severe biological response to worrying and anxiety than men do, according to this study.

As if we needed a brain scan to tell us this. It should be clear just by interacting with each other that men and women are not wired the same way. It's true, some small degree of these differences may be cultural, but ask any gynecologist and they'll tell you women are, at least physically and hormonally, *significantly* different from men. It's only reasonable that these differences would translate into mental and emotional differences as well. Countless studies have proven these differences. This isn't a one-way street, of course. Women have their weaknesses, but they're also fantastic at many things men aren't naturally inclined to do.

I've heard some bitter women say this negative treatment of men is justified vengeance due to how women have been treated in the past—that it's natural for the pendulum to swing so far the other direction after years of misogyny. Sure, there have been bad men throughout all the ages, but there have always been bad women in the world as well. Any feminist who claims all or most of the ills in this world were done at the hands of men is the very picture of sexist. This supposed pendulum swing isn't right, and it isn't justified. To tear down the man in order to lift up the woman is extraordinarily offensive to both genders. And because the two genders are fundamentally connected, to tear down the man *is* to tear down the woman.

Where do we get off treating men this way? Who are our soldiers, policemen, leaders, explorers, risk-takers, firemen, patriarchs, protectors, entrepreneurs, breadwinners, physical laborers, hunters, strategists and analytical thinkers? These are all skills and areas which, compared to women, men are consistently superior. Our society thoroughly depends on good men, good fathers, and good husbands. We need men who are strong, courageous, driven, protective, intelligent, chivalrous, benevolent, bold, paternal, righteous, gentlemanly, hard-working, valiant, integrous, responsible, ambitious, honest, and diligent. All men have these elements of true manhood within them. If we are to save the world, we need these unapologetically masculine men. Masculinity is not a dirty word; it's just as beautiful and necessary as femininity.

If men as a whole aren't living up to these ideals, perhaps feminist society is partly to blame. Just as feminism is stifling a woman's inherent gifts, they're stifling a man's gifts as well. As a woman, I will wholeheartedly admit that the lack of male chivalry in this world is largely because of us. For one, feminists have told men everything about true manhood is offensive. And secondly, because many of us women aren't acting in the ladylike manner that would warrant gentlemanly treatment. I'm in no way suggesting that gentlemanly treatment needs to be earned by women—far from it. Chivalry and gentlemanly manners toward a woman are a reflection of the man, not the woman. But it is to say that it becomes easier and more natural for a man to be a gentleman around a lady who has proper respect and decorum in return. We can help bring out the best in men by bringing out the best in ourselves. I believe that if we as women act like ladies and learn to celebrate chivalry whenever possible, we have a real chance of turning things around. After all, we can't save the world without saving both the woman *and* the man.

# FEMINIST FAIRY TALE

## THE PRINCESS WHO COULDN'T BE TIED DOWN

ONCE upon a time, there was a ~~beautiful princess~~ strong, independent woman who had ~~a kind, loving disposition toward all her animal friends~~ career aspirations.

This strong, independent woman didn't need marriage or children because she was too logical for such nonsense. She had more important things to do, like ~~spreading joy and love~~ empowering herself through making lots of money. Princes and little royal children were not a priority. In fact, they would just hold her back from rising to her true potential. That's what she learned from modern-day feminism, after all.

So she worked hard in school and was accepted into a prestigious university. Again, she worked hard, getting exceptional grades and making all sorts of valuable connections. She was going to rule the world. There was no stopping her!

Until she began to long for a male connection. That's odd. She was always told she could do it on her own. But she wasn't worried. She just needed to get it out of her system so she could go back to being strong and independent. So she found a man who she used for a little while until he got in the way of her career goals, then she cut ties.

As she tried to re-focus on her career and shake off the emptiness inside, she was surprised with ~~true love's kiss~~ a positive pregnancy test.

The strong, independent woman was terrified. She didn't have time for a baby! She had too many other important things to do. This would ruin her plans and destroy her future. So she decided to destroy the baby's future instead. She had an abortion.

Now that the inconvenience was out of the way, she was free to pursue her ~~happily ever after~~ career goals again.

The strong, independent woman graduated college and immediately landed her dream job. As a hobby, she also became an online fitness guru, inspiring thousands of women to lead healthy lifestyles. She even began educating other women about how they could be independent and empowered as well. Her life was exactly as she had always dreamed.

But she wasn't happy. She couldn't figure out why. She had done everything she needed to do in life to be fulfilled, yet her life felt empty.

Years passed and she began to age. As she grew into her fifties, the hard reality that she would never have another child began to sink in, and her choice to abort the one she did conceive began to eat her up at night. Who would that child be by now? What would it have felt like to hold that baby and watch him or her grow up? Would that son or daughter have discovered the cure for cancer? Would they have become president? Would they have helped people? Had their own children? Brought a little more light into this dark world? Supported her in her old age? Loved her even when everyone else abandoned her?

On her deathbed, the strong, independent woman began to wonder if "independent" was just another word for lonely. She no longer cared about her money or worldly achievements. All she cared about was the empty room. No husband. No children. No grandchildren. No legacy and no one to mourn her death.

At least she had that degree on her wall.

~~And she lived happily ever after.~~

# 6

## THE CASE FOR WOMEN TO BE HOMEMAKERS

WOMEN are strong. Women are capable. Women are talented. Women are incredibly important to the family and, by extension, to the world.

With that in mind, do me a favor: imagine a little boy right now. Not one who's screaming or throwing a temper tantrum, but a little toddler, fresh out of the bathtub, quietly sitting in your lap. Imagine the way he smells, his softness, his warmth. Now picture him turning his head and gazing up at you. His big, innocent eyes stare at you with curiosity and wonder. He's amazed by you. As he should be. After all, you're the reason he's alive. You gave birth to him. You feed him. You keep him safe. You teach him. You comfort him. You're his hero. You have the power to guide his destiny to something absolutely incredible or, potentially, to something tragic. To this one little person, you are the world.

You are a mother. Can you name another job as vital to our future—as vital to the human race's very existence?

I think C.S. Lewis said it best: "The homemaker has the ultimate career. All other careers exist for one purpose only - and that is to support the ultimate career."

Being a wife and mother *is* the ultimate career. This is the very reason *women* have specifically been entrusted with the sacred responsibility of bearing and rearing children: precisely *because* women are strong, capable, and talented. After all, who better to take on the "ultimate career" than a strong, capable, and talented woman?

This chapter is our plea to every mother in the world to consider giving up her desk and cubicle for something infinitely more meaningful and necessary.

Before we go any further, a disclaimer: *the writers of this book understand it's not possible for every woman to quit her job, namely single mothers. The writers of this book do not judge or condemn women who choose to work outside the home, for whatever reason.* We understand everyone is different and everyone's situation is unique. The purpose of this chapter is simply to illustrate the benefits of full-time motherhood and the disadvantages of partial motherhood, and to persuade those who can stay home to reach for that worthy goal. We believe there's nothing more empowering than motherhood done correctly. Some women may *think* it's impossible for them to leave their jobs because they've been taught by feminism that they can't survive without certain material things, when in reality, they could be just as happy (if not more so) living on only one income. Downsizing a home, a car, going out to eat less, learning to budget more effectively, learning to sew and other self-reliance skills etc. is well worth the long-term benefits of being an ever-present mother.

Without further ado, I'd like to make the case for women to be homemakers. Because there are so many members of the family this choice affects, I've broken it up into sections, starting with the littlest members.

## The Children

The term "latchkey kid" (a child who is unsupervised by an adult for at least part of the day, especially after returning home from school) was invented in World War II when many mothers had to go to work as a result of the war. Today, millions of children between the ages of five and twelve still come home to empty houses. What was then an unfortunate effect of war has now become the norm. The United States Department of

Labor reported that in 2012, 69.9% of all mothers work outside the home. Worse, 57.3% of mothers with *infant* children work outside the home, often leaving their children in daycare facilities during work hours. That's not only heartbreaking, it's destructive.

An extensive study conducted by Jay Belsky, a researcher on infant development, and David Eggebeen, an expert in health and human development, said this:

> Upon reviewing studies of maternal employment and of nonparental care involving infants, Belsky concluded that children who experienced 20 or more hours per week of nonparental care in their first year of life of the kind routinely available in the United States (often proxied by extensive maternal employment) are at the elevated risk of developing insecure attachments to their mothers... and of being more disobedient toward adults and aggressive toward peers as three-to-eight-year-olds… than other children.

Difficulty attaching and aggressive behavior isn't entirely surprising in children who have limited contact with their mothers, since mothers are typically the most calming and reassuring figures in a young child's life. *Time* elaborated on this idea with article on the study of young monkeys. The research group placed certain monkeys in normal environments with mothers, some in peer-reared groups, and others in complete isolation. These were their findings:

The results differed by gender, an effect also seen in humans suffering from child maltreatment. Male monkeys reared in isolation were nearly twice as likely to come down with physical illnesses as those reared by their mothers or with peers. They were also more than five times as likely to show stereotyped behavior, the repetitive motions similar to the rocking or head-banging seen in some cases of autism and in orphanage-reared infants. The peer-reared males were about three times more likely to engage in stereotyped behavior, compared with those raised by their mothers.

In females, surprisingly, the peer-reared group did worse than the monkeys raised in isolation. They were far more likely to be wounded and to suffer hair loss than monkeys raised by their mothers or in isolation. The researchers found that the peer-reared females were more aggressive than other monkeys, suggesting that the wounds may have resulted from fights and the hair loss from hair-pulling by others.

Peer-rearing in humans is often a result of children spending most of their waking hours in school or day-care where they learn mostly from other children. James Heckman, Nobel-prize-winning economist and one of the authors of the study, argued that investing time early on in a child's life is crucial. He said this study "shows that early life conditions critically affect adult health. Maternal attachment plays a fundamental role in shaping who we are; remove it and the harm is great."

Though the researchers were using these monkeys as a means to create parallels to children who grew up in orphanages, it's reasonable to apply their findings, to a lesser extent, to children who were, at least partially, raised in daycare facilities. The study outlined that children, just like the monkeys in the study, though their basic needs are taken care of, suffered emotionally, cognitively, and even physically well into adulthood because they did not experience *personalized* nurturing. The article had this to say about children who grew up in Romanian orphanages in the 80s and 90s:

> The longer these children were left in their cribs, simply being fed and changed without individualized affection, the more damage was seen, even if the orphanage was clean and well-run. Many children developed autistic-like behaviors, repetitively rocking or banging their heads. Some were cold

and withdrawn or indiscriminately affectionate; some alternated between these extremes. And they simply didn't grow like normal infants: their head circumferences were abnormally small and they had problems with attention and comprehension.

It's true, being in a daycare center for eight hours is not the same as living in an orphanage without any parents at all. However, eight hours is a huge percentage of the waking day and it would be unreasonable to overlook the lesser damage that could still occur by only having *part-time* parents. Pre-school and daycare, though they are well-meaning and sometimes necessary, are no substitutes for a mother who devotes all her time, energy, and love into her children. Yes, their physical needs are being met at these types of facilities, but they are being emotionally and spiritually neglected, which in turn, affects them both mentally and even physically. With the sudden spike of disorders like autism and ADHD, we should be looking into the possibility that these things are linked. Back in the 1940s, when autism was first being discovered, the term "refrigerator mother" was coined. It was a phrase used to describe mothers, or both parents, who were excessively cold toward their children. Leo Kanner, the psychiatrist and physician who first described autism, admitted this was one possible contributor to the disorder. In short, it was theorized that a lack of affection and warmth toward a child in his early years could produce serious mental and physical distress. Kanner later renounced the theory for unknown reasons, possibly due to societal pressure.

But what if, in certain cases, there is a link to limited parental time and autism? Autism has gone from being nearly unheard of in the 1940s to a world-wide epidemic, particularly in the United States, in about seventy years. This is partially due to the fact that we've gotten better at diagnosing it, but that can't completely account for the 78% increase in autism in the past twelve years or the 30% increase in just the past two. Certainly there are many factors involved in a complex disorder such as autism, and again, correlation doesn't always equal causation, but we have to notice the rise of autism has paralleled closely with the steep rise of single motherhood and part-time motherhood.

A recent HealthDay News study that shows adult autism patients benefited greatly from the hormone oxytocin. Oxytocin is also known as "the love hormone" or "the bonding hormone" because it's released in the brain when one gives or receives love. It's the hormone that begins uterus contractions during labor, and it's said the reason a mother falls in love with her newborn baby so instantaneously is because she's full of this hormone immediately after giving birth. Oxytocin is shown to be released between a mother and child when mothers breastfeed, give hugs, and give other types of affection. It plays a massive role in the emotional bond between mother and child. The adult autism patients who were given just *one* dose of synthetic oxytocin "quickly improved their ability to judge facial expressions and emotions."

What a fantastic discovery! If this synthetic hormone, the hormone that should naturally occur in any healthy parent-child relationship, has the ability to improve an adult with autism, can you imagine what receiving healthy doses of this hormone *naturally* would do for a *child* with autism? Could it possibly lower the risk of it occurring to begin with? I'm no doctor, but perhaps it's something to consider.

The emotional, mental, and physical benefits of having a mother present and attentive are undeniable. Every mother wants to be close to her children and every child craves it as well. This doesn't end when children start school. The constant need for a mother at home continues well into their teenage years, when it's arguably most important to be there to help guide their decisions and give them emotional support. Though the negative results of having an absent mother when infants are involved is much more dramatic, children and even teenagers without a mother at home can also suffer crippling consequences. The impacts of emotional neglect can result in anti-social behaviors, delinquency, teenage pregnancy, depression, anxiety, self-esteem issues, etc.

Many mothers justify their choices to work outside the home by saying it's actually *good* for their kids—that it teaches them independence and shows their daughters, by example, that they can be anything they want to be. There may be some truth to this. However, I contend the greater message being sent is that the child comes second in the mother's life. I'd be willing to wager the majority of those kids would rather spend more time with their mothers than have more "stuff." Working mothers everywhere say things like "I just want to give my children more than I had," but what are they *really* giving them? Money? Is that more important than time? We send mothers away, abandoning their families for the sole purpose of making *money*, yet we complain that this rising generation is so materialistic. We've been teaching our children by example that money is more important than family and the only way for them to be happy and "find themselves" is to put distance between themselves and the people they love.

Children are entitled to a mother who is present. Children have complex and highly individual needs. There is only one person qualified to fill these needs, and that is his mother.

## The Men

Besides the gender-role-confusion we talked about earlier, when women collectively enter the workforce, it also negatively affects men financially.

Let's look at the numbers. In 2010, women comprised about 47% of the total labor force—a labor force that was almost entirely male-dominated just a hundred years earlier.

*Well, great! We must be making more money due to more employed people per household!*

Not exactly. Yes, it's true we're making a little more money than in the past, but this has nothing to do with women working. As you can see by the graph below, having more women in the workforce actually has little-to-nothing to do with household income increases. The numbers don't seem to correlate at all.

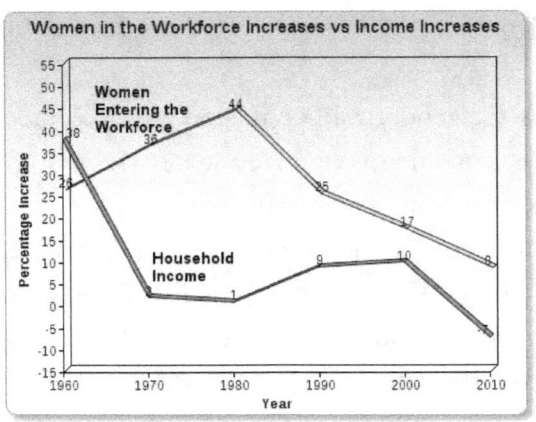

Women in the Workforce Increases vs Income Increases

[adjusted for inflation]

If having more two-source income families increased income, these lines should be fairly parallel. But, as you can see, the year we had the biggest spike in women entering the workforce was around 1980. This was also the year with one of the *lowest* increases to total household income, with an increase of little more than 1%. In short, more women working doesn't necessarily mean household income increases.

How does that make sense? More women working should mean a bigger household income, right? Well, a dramatic rise in single-motherhood may be a big factor in driving household incomes down. It may also be partly due to the fact that as women decided to start working, men's wages declined. It stands to reason. The amount of labor was being handled just fine by men in the past, so when women began entering the force, the

110

work suddenly needed to be divided between the sexes. The workforce became more competitive, and one-person jobs were being split into two-person jobs. But employers couldn't afford to pay two people for the same amount of work one person used to do. So the wages, along with the work, were being shared. Don't believe me? Take a look at this chart showing income levels for men and women ages 35-44:

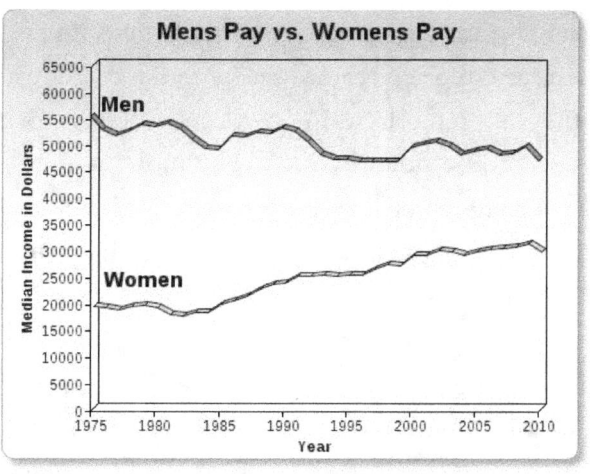

[adjusted for inflation]

First of all, yes, there *appears* to be a gap in wages between men and women, but as we covered earlier, looks can be deceiving. What's really important to look at here is this: women's median income has been steadily increasing since the seventies, going up from $18,985 to $30,061—a 58% increase (adjusted for inflation). Yay us, I guess. Though that really just means we're working more hours now. Adjusted for inflation, this is about a $12,000 increase in women's income. But where did that extra $12,000 come from? Well, men's income has been tipping downward, falling from $55,569 in the early seventies to $45,224 in 2012—that's roughly a $10,000 dollar *drop*. The difference is even more drastic when you look at the income of younger men whose income has fallen even further. There are a limited number of jobs available in the market, so unless each woman entering the workforce starts her own business, and the vast majority do not, they are filling positions that used to be filled by men. The more women go to work, the more the income of men as a whole drops and the more of them are put out of work entirely. It's simple math.

The only party that benefits by having two sources of income in each home is, as always, the government. Taxes have been raised significantly since the dawn of the working woman lifestyle. It seems any significant extra income a family would make by having two employed members is now going straight to the government. After all, the IRS now has *two* taxable incomes per home. This is just one reason the government loves feminism. And for those who are still trying to make it on only one source of income, this adds severe financial strain.

This competing between the genders for jobs also forces both parties to shill out more money for more education in an attempt to set themselves apart, which causes an unnecessarily cut-throat work environment where people are fearful of losing their jobs. And for good reason, considering unemployment is at record highs.

Not only does this mainstream idea that women need to be in the workforce negatively affect finances, but it affects the workplace environment as well. I'm going to recount a personal story to which I'd wager many of you can relate.

The two authors of this book used to work in a large office together. During that time, we became acquainted with a nineteen-year-old girl who we affectionately called Spongebob Squarehead because of the way she teased her hair into a perfect, gravity-defying square every day.

For several months, the author who sat next to this woman endured all kinds of horrific torture. Alright, maybe not quite *torture*, but close enough. Everything from constant chip crunching and the leaving of garbage and crumbs all over the shared desk, to the attempts to chat with the author while on business calls—usually about her favorite boy of the day. Not to mention, the daily hairspray in the face. Yes, she not only did all of her makeup at her desk each morning (after coming in late), but she also did her trademark hairdo right next to this author. This often meant a good thirty minutes of teasing, spraying, repeat. And the big balls of hair or, more accurately, small cats that were torn out during this ritual? The author was unfortunate enough to regularly get them caught in the wheels of her chair. Worst of all, near the end of the day this girl would often decide she needed to air-out her sweaty feet and take off her shoes. This is when she'd kick her bare feet onto the shared desk, dangerously close to this author's face.

This was a fairly classy office with a strict dress-code. It was perplexing that she was able to get away with breaking so many rules right in front of the supervisor. Said supervisor, a middle-aged man—let's call him Mr. Midlife Crisis—was one of the most respected supervisors in the whole company. He was extremely hard on all of his team, yet Squarehead was allowed to be late virtually every day without any repercussions whatsoever. This continued for months, all the while, she was blatantly unworried about her job security.

None of this made sense until news broke of what was occurring after work hours—and even *during* work hours. Mr. Crisis was having an affair with Squarehead. In fact, they were caught "in the act" by some poor, unsuspecting employee in the stairwell one day. Thank goodness this author took the elevator.

Mr. Crisis was immediately fired, as he should have been. But Squarehead? She got to keep her job. And after this scandal came to light, Squarehead's special treatment continued. In fact, during the course of these escapades, she had become pregnant by Mr. Crisis and the company rewarded her with paid leave to appease her while she took care of the situation. No one else was entitled to that, but the company complied with her for fear of being sued.

Now, in situations such as this, feminists will immediately point the finger at the man, insisting he was more at fault than the woman because he was her professional superior and therefore held more "power."

But was that *really* the case? I would argue Squarehead held more power—so much power that it turned a respected married man with two kids into a slave to nothing more than her body. After this woman played a major role in breaking another woman's heart, tearing apart a family, and causing a man to lose his job, she had the nerve to brag about the whole thing like it was some sort of badge of honor. She knew *exactly* what she was doing all along. It had been initiated by her. And still, she kept her job.

As mentioned earlier, women have *always* had power. It reminds me of a line from the 2002 romantic comedy, *My Big Fat Greek Wedding*: "Let me tell you something, Toula. The man is the head, but the woman is the neck. And she can turn the head any way she wants."

Whether we decide to use this power for good or for evil is entirely up to us. This woman in this story used it to not only secure her position but to gain an absurd amount of special treatment. The fault belongs to both her and the supervisor equally, but only one party was punished.

Unfortunately, this isn't an isolated incident. I'd be willing to bet many reading this have experienced similar tragedies at their own jobs. This is a workplace epidemic. Women using their bodies to gain power and men using their power to gain, well… bodies.

Feminism has resulted in women making up half the current workforce when it used to be almost completely male dominated. Now, for the first time ever, married men are in close proximity to women who aren't their wives for eight hours a day, five days a week—women who are on their best behavior and dressed to impress. And, suddenly, these women are more attractive and interesting than their wives—wives who are at home, makeup-less, wearing yoga pants, and covered in baby vomit. The problem is: these men are only attracted to their female co-worker's *false personas* because they never see them outside of work. Unlike with their wives, they never see these women at their worst. These workplace relationships are based on lies.

Not only that, but the men begin to have more in common emotionally with these women because of similar work histories, talents, interests, and shared experiences. How can a housewife compete with all of this?

It's not a one-way street—the same thing happens to women. It makes sense. After all, they're constantly around these men during work hours, breaks, lunches, company parties, business trips, etc. Even if the two parties don't actually have a physical relationship, they begin to become best friends. They spend time with, flirt, and confide in one another.

This is becoming so widespread that there's actually a term for it: the "work spouse." It's been talked about on Dr. Phil, CNN, The Huffington Post, even WebMD. Long story short, men and women are spending so much time together in the office that they consciously or subconsciously seek out a second spouse, one for work-time only. Some see this as completely normal—something we should just accept. But it's *not* normal. It's destructive and nothing more than emotional cheating. And it's a problem for marriages, considering 65% of women find an emotional affair more hurtful than a sexual affair.

We should have seen this coming. In the grand scheme of things, the "work spouse" is an extremely new issue, something no previous generation had to

117

worry about. Now, it's destroying marriages right and left and making it very uncomfortable for other employees who are caught in the middle.

## The Women

We've already touched on the fact that women aren't naturally inclined to work the same way men are. We've found that women miss more hours of work on average even when they don't have children. We talked about how women still do more housework than men even when they work the same number of hours outside the home, and about how confused gender roles can break down marriages. But how does it affect a woman's psyche when she feels pressured to "do it all"?

In this modern era, women have more freedom, more rights, and more opportunities than ever before. Women can do what they want, say what they want, and be whatever they want. Women can marry, have kids, have a career, all of the above, some of the above, or none of the above. As mentioned earlier, if this was indeed the true goal of feminism, then feminism has won. Woman officially has all the same rights as man. Women are in powerful positions, running large corporations, making history, setting world-records, having their voices heard and their names renowned all over the world. Taking all of this into account, in the year

2014, women *should* be happier than ever in recorded history. Right? Unfortunately, this is not the case.

*We're strong! We're independent! We're... miserable.*

Depression, anxiety, addiction, and suicide are on the rise among women. While suicide rates are up for both middle-aged genders, a 40% increase from 1999 to 2010, women now attempt suicide three times as often as men. Addiction among women, especially addiction to painkillers and tranquilizers, is on a steep incline. Countries where women have the most opportunities are also the countries with the most alcoholism and drug abuse among women. Regarding depression, a study highlighted on Forbes.com said this:

> Conflicts between family and work influenced depression risk for both sexes, but in different ways. Men were at increased risk of depression if their family life got in the way of their work life, while women were at increased risk of depression if their work life interfered with their family life.

Let's face it, work life *always* interferes with family life. Our inherent roles clearly play a part in our happiness. Economists Betsey Stevenson and Justin Wolfers wrote at length about this subject, acquiring and analyzing data from various demographics, in their working paper entitled *The Paradox of Declining Female Happiness*. In the past 35 years, their findings show:

> [W]omen in the United States have become less happy, both absolutely and relative to men. Women have traditionally reported higher levels of happiness than men, but they are now reporting happiness levels that are similar or even lower than those of men. The relative decline in well-being holds across various datasets, and holds whether one asks about happiness or life satisfaction.

They go on to say:

> [T]rends in self-reported subjective well-being indicate that happiness has shifted toward men and away from women. This shift holds across industrialized countries regardless of whether the aggregate trend in happiness for both genders is flat, rising, or falling: in all of these cases we see happiness rebalancing to reflect greater happiness for men relative to women.

Why are women less happy now than they were 35 years ago?

Being a woman sucks sometimes. Women, among their many good traits, usually come with sadness-inducing traits like perfectionism. This is why women don't like letting men fold the laundry because they just don't *do* it right. A woman likes to be in control of the situation, and when a chore isn't being done, a woman is the first to pick up the slack and do it herself. And a woman is never happy until things are done perfectly because, if they're not, it brings on another of a woman's curses: insecurity. Women constantly beat themselves up about one thing or another. This is why women have body image issues. A woman looks at a Photoshopped magazine model or a surgically altered actress followed by a team of makeup artists and perpetually good lighting and she thinks, "Why don't I look like her?" She begins to think less of herself because one thing women are really great at is comparing every aspect of their lives to every aspect of *other* women's lives. Even more irrationally, a woman typically compares her *worst* to their *best*. The beauty industry and Hollywood are only partially to blame. The issue runs much deeper than that. This perfectionism and insecurity is, unfortunately, a shared weakness in most of the female race. Ban Photoshop and hair extensions and women will find other ways to compare themselves to other women.

In the past, all a woman had to compare to others was the one job: her home and family. She put all her time and effort into making those things the best they could be; she made her home the prettiest, made her children the best-behaved, cooked the best meals, and so on.

Nowadays, however, she sees Mrs. Doitall down the street doing it all: home, family, a fancy career; and she even finds time to work out and get her nails done. On the outside, her life looks absolutely perfect. But that's the thing: other women only *see* the outside. They don't realize how much Mrs. Doitall's private life is falling apart at the seams. Maybe it is, maybe it isn't, but the woman observing from the outside doesn't care. She only compares the external things. In their quest to do it all, other women begin following suit and, suddenly, our insecure stay-at-home mom is the only non-career woman on the block. She begins to wonder if she's doing enough. She sees her husband collapse on the couch after work, emotionally exhausted and his back aching. He may even worry aloud about finances, which she instantly takes to heart. *"Maybe he's working too hard because I'm not working hard enough,"* she thinks. *"Maybe I should be doing more like Mrs. Doitall. Maybe I'm not pulling my weight. Oh, my gosh. Maybe I need to LOSE weight!"*

You get the point. Before she knows it, she's been sucked in. Now she's got yet another job—one outside the home—and suddenly she's doing it all too. Except she's not, because it's not physically possible to put her heart, time, and energy into *everything*. One or more areas will always suffer. She will try to hide it the best she can from the other do-it-all women. She will even try to hide it from herself. But something will suffer and, most likely, it's going to be everything. Taking on more responsibilities did nothing to alleviate her guilt or insecurities. And through it all, she can't understand why she's not feeling happy or "fulfilled" like the feminists promised.

Author, Anne Morrow Lindbergh, made this observation:

The Feminists did not look ... far [enough] ahead; they laid down no rules of conduct. For them it was enough to demand the privileges. ... And [so] woman today is still searching. We are aware of our hunger and needs, but still ignorant of what will satisfy them. With our garnered free time, we are more apt to drain our creative springs than to refill them. With our pitchers [in hand] we attempt ... to water a field, [instead of] a garden. We throw ourselves indiscriminately into the committees and causes. Not knowing how to feed the spirit, we try to muffle its demands in distractions. Instead of stilling the center, the axis of the wheel, we add more centrifugal activities to our lives—which tend to throw us [yet more] off balance.

Mechanically we have gained, in the last generation, but spiritually we have ... lost."

Feminism has used a woman's weakness against herself. Countless doors with various different life paths have been laid out before each woman for generations. If she wanted a career, she could pass through that door. If she wanted a family, she could pass through that one. If she wanted an education, she could pass through that, or a hundred other different kinds of doors. Most women however, passed through the door to which they naturally gravitated: a door entitled "Marriage and Family." And there's nothing to indicate any previous generation regretted that choice. If we were to ask our mothers, grandmothers, or great-grandmothers how they felt about their decision to become homemakers, I'd bet most would say it was the most rewarding, fulfilling, difficult, but joyful path they could've taken.

Today, feminism hasn't created more doors, for they always existed. Rather, feminism has opened every door wide and placed neon signs pointing to each of them. It's told women that they're not doing enough to be happy unless they pass through *every* door, even traditionally male doors. At the same time, feminism discourages the tried and true "Marriage and Family" door unless the woman has already passed through all the others first. Feminism has led women to believe that they must prove they can be men before they're allowed to be women. A woman is so desperate to please, eager to do anything she can to ultimately take the path she wants to take, that she jumps through all the hoops. She ends up doing it all. And now, women are not only comparing themselves to other women, but to men. This will drive women to insecurity quicker than anything else as they're now encouraged, and even forced, to compete with men in their inherent *male* strengths.

In order to compete with men, women must by necessity take on characteristics of men. Generally speaking, men are more aggressive, confident, and competitive, so now, the "gentler sex" has been forced to become, well, ungentle. A woman in the workplace learns quickly that natural feminine traits are liabilities. *"You can't just give food away because the customer was short on the bill,"* her restaurant manager says. *"Don't let them see you cry or they'll think you can't handle the promotion,"* says her co-worker. *"Be more assertive!"* her sales manager says, *"You have to put more pressure on the caller if you want to keep up with the rest of the team."* In order to move up in the company, or even just keep her current job, a woman consciously or subconsciously begins to take on male characteristics, thus suppressing her femininity.

We see the effects of it every day on the news and in our own communities: the disturbing increase of teenage girls getting into physical fights, the growing number of women in our jail systems (from 2000 to 2009, the number of women incarcerated increased over 20% compared to an increase of about 15% for men), and the general harshness of women in word and deed. Softness and kindness, when it comes to females, are seen as weaknesses. Because of this, women have been forced to take into repression, holding back natural tears and emotions in an effort to appear "strong." This is a danger to not only a woman's sanity but to the world.

Is it any wonder the world is in chaos and war when society is constantly suffocating natural feminine traits such as compassion, meekness, empathy, submissiveness, spirituality, and gentleness? Good femininity is absolutely crucial to balancing the world's widespread anger. The world is crying out for a mother's nurturing love, a wife's tender support, a sister's gentle words, a grandmother's warm hugs. I contend that what happens in the home has always been the most vital ingredient in any good work that has ever been performed. Religious leader, Neil A. Maxwell, summed it up when he posed these thought-provoking questions:

When the real history of mankind is fully disclosed, will it feature the echoes of gunfire or the shaping sound of lullabies? The great armistices made by military men or the peacemaking of women in homes and in neighborhoods? Will what happened in cradles and kitchens prove to be more controlling than what happened in congresses?

Yes, I believe it will. More mothers must reclaim their homes, cultivating their natural strengths and talents, but there's also a behavior and mindset restoration that needs to take place. Margaret D. Nadauld said it perfectly:

The world has enough women who are tough; we need women who are tender. There are enough women who are coarse; we need women who are kind. There are enough women who are rude; we need women who are refined. We have enough women of fame and fortune; we need more women of faith. We have enough greed; we need more goodness. We have enough vanity; we need more virtue. We have enough popularity; we need more purity.

When women are forced into a competitive work environment, it's not possible to become those women. Because of this, it's absolutely crucial to reject the female career expectations and instead, allow women to get in touch with these ideal traits once again. The happiness and wellbeing of the female race depends upon it.

At the conclusion of their report, Stevenson and Wolfers summarized their findings about female happiness:

> Finally, the changes brought about through the women's movement may have decreased women's happiness. The increased opportunity to succeed in many dimensions may have led to an increased likelihood of believing that one's life is not measuring up. Similarly, women may now compare their lives to a broader group, including men, and find their lives more likely to come up short in this assessment. Or women may simply find the complexity and increased pressure in their modern lives to have come at the cost of happiness.

More opportunities, more freedom—that's great. More unfulfilling  work, more feelings of inferiority, more squashing of femininity, more depression... that's not as great.

What's the solution? Society must stop stigmatizing homemakers. We need to promote marriage. We need to create wholesome media and entertainment without feminist propaganda. We need to place the housewife back in her rightful, elect position as the ideal and then not judge another woman for her unique circumstances that may call her elsewhere. We need to stop pressuring everyone to do everything—men included. We need women to act like ladies again. We need to let women know that it's not just *okay* to spend more time with her children, but it's *good* for the children—it's something both parties desperately need and are being deprived of on a massive scale. Encouraging women to hone their natural abilities within the family is the best thing we could possibly do for women.

# Feminist Fairy Tale

## The Chief Executive Princess

ONCE upon a time, there was a strong, independent woman who was so strong that even though she was a woman and had the added disadvantage of being from a foreign country, she was able to achieve greatness in America. She graduated college with a Bachelor's degree in Physics, Chemistry, and Math, and went on to get her Master's in Finance and Marketing in her native country. After that, she moved to the United States where she earned her Master's in Public and Private Management at Yale.

From that point on, she worked her way up through a number of prominent companies, working hard and greatly benefiting each of them.

Somewhere in the middle of all this, the woman married, and she and her husband had two daughters. She didn't see this as a problem because feminism taught her that women can "have it all."

And she tried to have it all. Unfortunately, her job didn't leave much time for her family. She was constantly busy with her work—even going so far as to regularly have her kids call her secretary to ask permission when they wanted to play video games. The secretary would read through a list of questions, i.e. "Did you finish your homework?" If they answered yes, they were given permission by her secretary to play. It wasn't an ideal system, but it got the job done.

As time went on, however, her daughters began to feel their mother's absence more profoundly, frequently complaining that their mother was one of the only parents not present at certain mother-daughter events and school functions. They were beginning to feel abandoned. The mother felt guilty for not being there, and tried to justify her actions by reminding her children that other moms weren't always there for their kids either. It didn't help. It wasn't possible to make time for her kids with her hectic schedule. She was needed in too many places.

The woman eventually became the CEO of the fourth largest Food and Beverage company in the world, making her the 12th highest paid corporate woman in America and placing her in 100 Most Powerful Women lists and twice earning her the title of *Fortune*'s Most Powerful Business Woman in the world, just to name a few of her achievements.

No doubt this woman was extremely accomplished. But did she live happily ever after? Let's find out in her own words.

The above story is not fiction. It's the true story of Indra Nooyi, CEO of PepsiCo. In an interview with The Atlantic entitled "Why PepsiCo CEO Indra K. Nooyi Can't Have It All," Indra opened up about her guilt for neglecting her family, and explained why it's not possible for women to "have it all." She said this:

> I don't think women can have it all. I just don't think so. We pretend we *have* it all. We pretend we *can* have it all. My husband and I have been married for 34 years. And we have two daughters. And every day you have to make a decision about whether you are going to be a wife or a mother, in fact many times during the day you have to make those decisions. And you have to co-opt a lot of people to help you. We co-opted our families to help us. We plan our lives meticulously so we can be decent parents. But if you ask our daughters, I'm not sure they will say that I've been a good mom. I'm not sure. And I try all kinds of coping mechanisms.

Coping mechanisms like calling the school to find out how many other mothers also had to miss out at school functions and having her secretary handle video game playtime. She goes on:

> My observation... is that the biological clock and the career clock are in total conflict with each other. Total, complete conflict. When you have to have kids you have to build your career. Just as you're rising to middle management your kids need you because they're teenagers, they need you for the teenage years... And as you grow even more, your parents need you because they're aging. So we're screwed... [W]e cannot have it all.

Not only did her kids and aging parents suffer, but her husband also felt the effects. She continued:

> The person who hurts the most through this whole thing is your spouse. There's no question about it. You know, Raj always said, you know what, your list is PepsiCo, PepsiCo, PepsiCo, our two kids, your mom, and then at the bottom of the list is me.

Regardless of Indra's accomplishments, it's clear by her words that she's not happy with the huge sacrifices this choice has required. She continued by saying the fact that she had to miss out on so much time with her family makes her "die with guilt." Which begs the question:

maybe an executive career path is not the feminist dream it's been made out to be.

Clearly, women *can* have promising careers, run large corporations, and even entire countries, but the real question is: *should* we? Shouldn't women at least be presented with all the possible consequences before making a decision as important as this? Especially with feminists spewing the lie that "women can have it all," leading working women to question why their families are falling apart, why their health is suffering, and why they don't feel fulfilled.

It's not physically possible to throw one's time, energy, and heart into *everything* at once. The hard truth is: no matter what stage of life a woman is in, someone *always* needs her. She's naturally inclined to *want* to fill that need. The only solution is to drop what's least important and invest in what's most important. All of us, women and men alike, could benefit from reevaluating our list of priorities and ensuring our allotment of time aligns with those priorities.

# HOW TO SAVE THE WORLD

BEING a lady, saving the world… it's difficult, but it's not complicated. The goal is not to turn back the clock to the years of dowries and butter churning. The goal is to return to common sense, to value both genders equally, something that's unachievable while only promoting the wellbeing of one. This Frankenstein-like beast that is feminism has not only become something nearly impossible to define, but for decades, it's been actively damaging the human race.

Our goal is to encourage homemakers and full-time mothers to raise their voices, to be proud of what they've accomplished, and to not allow the world to shame them for their valiant sacrifices. Our goal is to return to the simple, ingenious system that's worked since the dawn of time—a system that has the potential to improve everyone's wellbeing by reducing the prevalence of all types of addiction, lowering the risk of mental disorders, promoting chivalry and ladylike behavior, ending the silent genocide that's eating away at our souls, creating more stable and healthy home environments, lowering divorce rates and reducing the number of single mothers, which as a result, would lower the prevalence of poverty, crime, delinquency, and all other types of damaging behavior. Transforming every family on earth into the strong support systems they were meant to be would have an astounding trickle up effect that could instantly solve the vast majority of the world's problems. That's the ultimate goal: to save the world.

We've done our best to lay out information from a side we don't normally hear in the media or the educational system. If you began reading this book as a critic, you've probably finished as one too, and that's fine. But to the young women who feel as I did in my teenage years and early twenties—women who have a deep, innate, unexplainable desire to be a mother, but feel pressured by society to follow another path: I want to let those women know that there is another option. Your teachers, your college professors, Hollywood, politicians, radicals, and even those close to you may tell you there's only one path—the path *they* choose for you. But you don't need to conform to the world's standard. Being a mother or a mother figure is more than enough. From the beginning of time, it's always been enough.

Isn't that what the feminist movement claims to be about? Defying cultural norms by following one's heart? If your heart is telling you to be a wife and mother—to throw your heart and soul into that "ultimate career" as C.S. Lewis called it, and sacrifice the more worldly rewards such as power, prestige, fame, and money for the priceless and everlasting blessing of a strong family unit—then the most "feminist" thing you can do is to follow those feelings. Be a mother to your own children or to others around you. Respect your body by dressing modestly. Be chaste and pure in deed, word, and thought. Create things of beauty. Speak only that which is true and uplifting. Embrace your sensitive and gentle nature. Lead your family beside a righteous husband. Be the virtuous, loving, compassionate lady you were born to be. None of these actions mean you're weak—on the contrary. They mean you're secure enough in your identity and your abilities that you don't need to prove you're valuable to the world. Your value shines through without you saying a word. Don't ever let others diminish who you are as a woman. You are God's crowning creation with sacred responsibilities entrusted only to women: to carry His children and give them life, to touch hearts, to nurture, and to create. What's more empowering than that?

To the men reading this book, we plead with you to allow women to be women. Encourage it. Embrace it. We need you as much as you need us. It's not sexist to want a woman who takes care of the home while you work to provide for the family. In fact, I'd be willing to bet most women secretly want to hear that from you.

The last thing we want to do is to make anyone feel guilty about the decisions they've made thus far, whatever those decisions may be. Heaven knows women carry around enough guilt as is. But wherever we are in life, it's never too late to make a change. However young or old we may be, however hopeless we may feel, however binding our situation may seem, we can start today by reevaluating our priorities. Do our priorities align with the time and energy we give to them each day? If not, maybe it's time for a change. We have a responsibility to our children and the future of the entire human race to correct those priorities. These problems aren't entirely our fault, but it does nothing productive to debate over who made the mess. We simply need to clean it up. We're women, after all. It's what we do.

We just have to save the world.

# CITATIONS

WE'VE ALWAYS HAD POWER:

**"In Diane Webb's book, The Forgotten Women of God"** Webb, Diana Barton. *Forgotten Women of God*. Bonneville Books, 2010.

**"k'enegdo"** Farrell, Heather. "The Real Meaning of the Term 'Help Meet.'" *Women in the Scriptures*, 2010, www.womeninthescriptures.com/2010/11/real-meaning-of-term-help-meet.html.

**"women who fall victim to things like honor killings"** "Honor Killing." *Wikipedia*. Wikimedia Foundation, 15 Apr. 2004. Web. 02 Aug. 2014. <http://en.wikipedia.org/wiki/Honor_killing>.

**"125 million women around the world who have to endure female genital mutilation"** "Female Genital Mutilation." *Wikipedia*. Wikimedia Foundation, 26 Oct. 2001. Web. 02 Aug. 2014. <http://en.wikipedia.org/wiki/Female_genital_mutilation>.

**"study performed by the Yerkes National Primate Center"** "Born This Way? Gender-Based Toy Preferences in Primates." *AnimalWise*. N.p., n.d. Web. 04 Aug. 2014. <http://animalwise.org/2012/01/26/born-this-way-gender-based-toy-preferences-in-primates/>.

FEMINISTS DON'T UNDERSTAND FEMINISM:

**"Google Ngram Viewer."** *Google Ngram Viewer*. N.p., n.d. Web. 24 Nov. 2014. <https://books.google.com/ngrams/graph?year_start=1800&year_end=2008&corpus=15&smoothing=7&case_insensitive=on&content=feminism>.

**"Many women held the right to vote in the United States as far back as the 1700s."** "The Woman Suffrage Timeline." *The Liz Library*. N.p., 1998. Web. 8 Sept. 2016. <http://www.thelizlibrary.org/suffrage/>.

**"William Bright, a saloonkeeper and member of his Wyoming city council…"** Klein, Christopher. "The State Where Women Voted Long Before the 19th Amendment." *History.com*. A&E Television Networks, 26 Aug. 2015. Web. 8 Sept. 2016.

<http://www.history.com/news/the-state-where-women-voted-long-before-the-19th-amendment>.

**"Others, including historian David Barton, have theorized…"** Mantyla, Kyle. "Barton: Not Allowing Women To Vote Was Designed 'To Keep The Family Together'" *Rightwingwatch.org*. People For the American Way, 1 May 2014. Web. 8 Sept. 2016.
<http://www.rightwingwatch.org/content/barton-not-allowing-women-vote-was-designed-keep-family-together>.

**"In fact, 15 states allowed women the right to vote before the 19th Amendment was ratified."** "Map: States Grant Women the Right to Vote." *Constitutioncenter.org*. National Constitution Center, 2006. Web. 8 Sept. 2016.
<http://constitutioncenter.org/timeline/html/cw08_12159.html>.

**"Feminists: Manipulated by Men Since 1929" (story of propagandist, Edward Bernays)** Curtis, Adam. "Happiness Machines." *The Century of Self*. BBC. United Kingdom, 17 Mar. 2002. *YouTube*. Web. 8 Sept. 2016.
<https://www.youtube.com/watch?v=eJ3RzGoQC4s>.

**"[smoking] now kills over 200,000 women a year."** "Tobacco-Related Mortality." *Cdc.gov*. Centers For Disease Control and Preventation, n.d. Web. 8 Sept. 2016.
<https://www.cdc.gov/tobacco/data_statistics/fact_sheets/health_effects/tobacco_related_mortality/>.

**"half of all smokers are now women…"** "Percent of Adults Who Smoke by Gender." *Kff.org*. Kaiser Family Foundation, n.d. Web. 8 Sept. 2016. <http://kff.org/other/state-indicator/smoking-adults-by-gen-der/?currentTimeframe=0&sortModel=%7B%22colId%22:%22Location%22,%22sort%22:%22asc%22%7D>.

**"Feminism, as defined by Merriam-Webster"** "Feminism." *Merriam-Webster*. Merriam-Webster, n.d. Web. 03 Aug. 2014.
<http://www.merriam-webster.com/dictionary/feminism>.

**"They brazenly march the streets, chanting and shouting, and carrying signs…"** Yoder, Katie, and Mairead Mcardle. "The 25 Craziest Pro-Abortion Signs Outside the Supreme Court Today." *LifeNews.com*. LifeNews.com, 2 Mar. 2016. Web. 8 Sept. 2016.
<http://www.lifenews.com/2016/03/02/the-25-craziest-pro-abortion-signs-outside-the-supreme-court-today/>.

**"'Abortion is a Civil Right.'"** "Brisbane, Austrailia." *40daysforlife.com*. 40 Days For Life, 22 Mar. 2015. Web. 8 Sept. 2016.
<https://40daysforlife.com/2015/03/22/brisbane-australia/>.

**"Can small minded idiot blokes…"** Mccormack, Kirsty. "'Can Idiot Blokes Stop Telling Women Whether They Are Entitled to Abortion': Pregnant Lily Allen Weighs into Row over 'women's Right to

Choose'" *Mail Online*. Associated Newspapers, 09 Oct. 2012. Web.
24 Nov. 2014. <http://www.dailymail.co.uk/tvshowbiz/article-
2215001/Lily-Allen-goes-Twitter-rant-adds-women-right-choose-
abortion.html>.

**"24 to 35% of men want to put more restrictions on abortion,
against 43 to 59% of women"** Robbins, Martin. "Why Are Wom-
en More Opposed to Abortion?" *Theguardian.com*. Guardian News
and Media, 30 Apr. 2014. Web. 07 Aug. 2014.
<http://www.theguardian.com/science/the-lay-
scientist/2014/apr/30/why-are-women-more-opposed-to-
abortion>.

**"slightly more men believe abortion should be 'generally available'
than women"** "Poll: Strong Support For Abortion Rights."
*CBSNews*. CBS Interactive. 22 Jan. 2003. Web. 07 Aug. 2014.
<http://www.cbsnews.com/news/poll-strong-support-for-
abortion-rights/>.

**"pro-choice and pro-life women are fairly evenly split down the
middle"** "U.S. Still Split on Abortion: 47% Pro-Choice, 46% Pro-
Life." *U.S. Still Split on Abortion: 47% Pro-Choice, 46% Pro-Life*. N.p.,
22 May. 2014. Web. 18 Aug. 2014.
<http://www.gallup.com/poll/170249/split-abortion-pro-choice-
pro-life.aspx>.

**"We now know that a bright flash of light occurs when the sperm
meets the egg..."** Knapton, Sarah. "Bright Flash of Light Marks
Incredible Moment Life Begins When Sperm Meets Egg." *Tele-
graph.co.uk*. Telegraph Media Group Limited, 26 Apr. 2016. Web. 8
Sept. 2016.
<http://www.telegraph.co.uk/science/2016/04/26/bright-flash-of-
light-marks-incredible-moment-life-begins-when-s/>.

**"We know that the heart begins beating at around five weeks..."**
"Fetal Development Week by Week." *Babycenter.com*. BabyCenter
L.L.C, n.d. Web. 8 Sept. 2016. <http://www.babycenter.com/fetal-
development-week-by-week>.

**"'punished with a baby'"** "President Obama: 'I Don't Want Them Punished With A Baby'" *YouTube*. YouTube, 27 Apr. 2011. Web. 23
Aug. 2014. <https://www.youtube.com/watch?v=jszkPtsFH-k>.

**"64% of women who had an abortion felt pressured to abort their
baby"** "Coerced or Forced Abortions in America." *Coerced or Forced
Abortions in America*. N.p., n.d. Web. 12 Aug. 2014.
<http://www.theunchoice.com/coerced.htm>.

**"'My first child was taken from me through the violence of Abor-
tion...'" "'I don't want to hide my child anymore.'" "'Having
an abortion was one of the hardest things I've ever done...'"
"'It still affects me every day of my life...'" "'Hurting and still
scared, I felt very abandoned...'" "'I was weeping and scream-**

143

ing, but nothing could turn back time.'" "Silent No More
Awareness Campaign: Testimony Directory." *Silent No More Awareness Campaign*. N.p., n.d. Web. 12 Aug. 2014.
<http://www.silentnomoreawareness.org/testimonies/index.aspx>.

**"Gianna Jessen, abortion survivor"** "Gianna Jessen." *Wikipedia*. Wikimedia Foundation, 15 May. 2005. Web. 18 Aug. 2014.
<http://en.wikipedia.org/wiki/Gianna_Jessen>.

**"'strangulation, suffocation, leaving the baby there to die, or throw-
ing the baby away.'"** "Gianna Jessen Abortion Survivor in Aus-
tralia Part 1." *YouTube*. YouTube, 10 Sept. 2008. Web. 12 Aug. 2014.
<https://www.youtube.com/watch?v=kPF1FhCMPuQ>.

**"'Today, a baby is a baby when convenient. It is tissue or otherwise
when the time is not right...'"** "AbortionFacts.com." *Gianna Jessen.*
N.p., n.d. Web. 12 Aug. 2014.
<http://www.abortionfacts.com/stories/gianna-jessen>.

**"57,107,921 just since the 70s"** "Number of Abortions - Abortion Coun-
ters." *Number of Abortions in US & Worldwide*. N.p., n.d. Web. 23
Aug. 2014. <http://www.numberofabortions.com/>.

**"'We should hire three or four colored ministers, preferably with
social-service backgrounds'"** "Margaret-Sanger & The Negro-
Project." *Margaret-Sanger & The Negro-Project*. N.p., n.d. Web. 14 Aug.
2014. <http://www.nationalblackprolifeunion.com/Margaret-
Sanger-and-The-Negro-Project.html>.

**"Considering black women are five times more likely to have an
abortion as white women and, though minority women are only 13% of the female population, minorities constitute 36% of
all abortions"**
"BlackGenocide.org | Abortion and the Black Community."
*BlackGenocide.org | Abortion and the Black Community*. Black-
Genocide.org, n.d. Web. 14 Sept. 2014.
<http://www.blackgenocide.org/black.html>.

**"Birth control must lead ultimately to a cleaner race"** "Margaret
Sanger." - *Wikiquote*. N.p., n.d. Web. 14 Aug. 2014.
<http://en.wikiquote.org/wiki/Margaret_Sanger>.

**"'more than 60,000 sterilizations of people considered 'feeble-
minded,' 'idiots' or 'morons.'"** "GROSSU: Margaret Sanger, Racist Eugenicist Extraordinaire." *Washington Times*. The Washington
Times, n.d. Web. 14 Aug. 2014.
<http://www.washingtontimes.com/news/2014/may/5/grossu-
margaret-sanger-eugenicist/>.

**"'A feminist is anyone who recognizes the equality and full humani-
ty of women and men.'"** "Women's and Gender Studies." *Quotes*.
N.p., n.d. Web. 13 Aug. 2014. <http://nau.edu/sbs/wgs/get-
involved/quotes/>.

**"flaunt an 'I had an abortion' T-shirt"** "'I Had an Abortion' Shirt Sales Stir Controversy at University of North Carolina Wilmington." *The Blaze*. TheBlaze Inc, 19 Apr. 2012. Web. 18 Aug. 2014. <http://www.theblaze.com/stories/2012/04/19/i-had-an-abortion-shirt-sales-stir-controversy-at-university-of-north-carolina-wilmington/>.

**"'From a public health point of view, abortion care, no less than contraception, is an essential measure to prevent the heart-break of infant mortality...'"** O'Neill, Terry. "Abortion, Like Con-traception, Is Essential Health Care That Saves Lives." *The Huffing-ton Post*. TheHuffingtonPost.com, 13 May 2014. Web. 18 Aug. 2014. <http://www.huffingtonpost.com/terry-oneill/abortion-like-contracepti_b_5316300.html>.

**"Hobby Lobby covers 16 of the 20 FDA approved forms of birth control"** "Is Hobby Lobby Really Banning Birth Control and Pre-venting Its Workers From 'Being Able to Make Their Own Health Care Decisions'?" *The Blaze*. TheBlaze Inc, 1 Jul. 2014. Web. 16 Aug. 2014. <http://www.theblaze.com/stories/2014/07/01/is-hobby-lobby-really-banning-birth-control-and-preventing-its-workers-from-being-able-to-make-their-own-health-care-decisions/>.

**"The Feminist Icon of Our Dreams"** Vagianos, Alanna. "Beyoncé Just Morphed Into The Feminist Icon Of Our Dreams." *The Huffington Post*. TheHuffingtonPost.com, 22 July 2014. Web. 26 Oct. 2014. <http://www.huffingtonpost.com/2014/07/22/beyonce-feminism-instagram-photo_n_5611112.html>.

**"push for gender neutral bathrooms"** "It's Time to End the Long His-tory of Feminism Failing Transgender Women." *Bitch Media*. N.p., 17 Jan. 2014. Web. 18 Aug. 2014. <http://bitchmagazine.org/post/the-long-history-of-transgender-exclusion-from-feminism>.

**"The 23-cent gender pay gap is simply the difference between the average earnings of all men and women working full-time..."** **"Women, on average, choose careers with lower pay..."** Som-mers, Christina Hoff. *The Daily Beast*. Newsweek/Daily Beast, 01 Feb. 2014. Web. 16 Aug. 2014. <http://www.thedailybeast.com/articles/2014/02/01/no-women-don-t-make-less-money-than-men.html>.

**"'Men [are] almost twice as likely as women to work more than 40 hours a week.'"** *The Wall Street Journal*. Dow Jones & Company, 07 Apr. 2014. Web. 16 Aug. 2014. <http://online.wsj.com/news/articles/SB1000142405270230353270457948375209957472>.

**"Women, on average, miss more work than men even when they don't have children."** "Female Absenteeism Is Not Just about Child Care." *Msnbc.com*. NBCNews.com, 05 Nov. 2007. Web. 16

Aug. 2014. <http://www.nbcnews.com/id/21547885/ns/business-careers/t/female-absenteeism-not-just-about-child-care/#.U-lxNbSK2M2>.

**"women call in sick about 189 times in a lifetime while men call in about 140 times"** Reporter, Daily Mail. "Pull the Other One: Women Call in Sick More Often, but Men Are More Likely to Skip Work as Soon as They Start Feeling Ill." *Mail Online.* Associated Newspapers, 25 May. 2011. Web. 16 Aug. 2014. <http://www.dailymail.co.uk/femail/article-1390371/Women-sick-men-skip-work-soon-start-feeling-ill.html>.

**"the massive 23-cent-gap, on average, shrinks all the way down to a miniscule... Five cents."** Sommers, Christina Hoff. *The Daily Beast.* Newsweek/Daily Beast, 01 Feb. 2014. Web. 16 Aug. 2014. <http://www.thedailybeast.com/articles/2014/02/01/no-women-don-t-make-less-money-than-men.html>.

**"men are more competitive and are more willing to ask for a raise than women"** "Salary, Gender and the Social Cost of Haggling." *Washington Post.* The Washington Post, 30 July 2007. Web. 18 Aug. 2014. <http://www.washingtonpost.com/wpdyn/content/article/2007/07/29/AR2007072900827.html>.

**"'No woman should be authorized to stay at home and raise her children...'"** Friedan, Betty. *It Changed My Life: Writings on the Women's Movement.* New York: Random House, 1976. 397. Print.

**"transgender women often believe they were born with a woman's brain inside a man's body. But on the other hand" "'I will not call a male "she"; thirty-two years of suffering...'" "'Anyone born a man retains male privilege in society...'"** "The Dispute Between Radical Feminism and Transgenderism." *The New Yorker.* N.p., 04 Aug. 2014. Web. 17 Aug. 2014. <http://www.newyorker.com/magazine/2014/08/04/woman-2>.

**"'acts of vandalism — stealing electrical cables, cutting water pipes, keying cars in the parking lot...'"** "Scenes from the Feminist Implosion." *New York Post.* NYP Holdings, 04 Aug. 2014. Web. 20 Aug. 2014. <http://nypost.com/2014/08/04/scenes-from-the-feminist-implosion/>.


THE WAR ON MARRIAGE:


**"We have to abolish and reform the institution of marriage"** "Rape=Marriage?" *What Liberals Say RSS.* N.p., n.d. Web. 21 Aug. 2014. <http://www.aim.org/wls/category/marriage/>.

**"A liberated woman is one who has sex before marriage and a job after."** "A Quote by Gloria Steinem." *Goodreads.* N.p., n.d. Web. 21

Aug. 2014. <https://www.goodreads.com/quotes/61054-a-liberated-woman-is-one-who-has-sex-before-marriage>.

"The complete destruction of traditional marriage and the nuclear family is the 'revolutionary or utopian' goal of feminism." "The Howard Center: The Religion & Society Report." *The Howard Center: The Religion & Society Report*. N.p., n.d. Web. 21 Aug. 2014. <http://profam.org/pub/rs/rs_2207.htm>.

"We can't destroy the inequities between men and women until we destroy marriage." "The Feminists." *Wikipedia*. Wikimedia Foundation, 19 Jan. 2006. Web. 21 Aug. 2014. <http://en.wikipedia.org/wiki/The_Feminists>.

"Since marriage constitutes slavery for women..." Sheila Cronan, in *Radical Feminism* - "Marriage" (1970), Koedt, Anne, Ellen Levine, and Anita Rapone. New York: Quadrangle, 1973. 219. Print.

"Marriage as an institution developed from rape as a practice." "Andrea Dworkin - Discover the Networks." *Andrea Dworkin - Discover the Networks*. N.p., n.d. Web. 21 Aug. 2014. <http://www.discoverthenetworks.org/individualProfile.asp?indid =1951>.

"Marriage has existed for the benefit of men..." "Rape=Marriage?" *What Liberals Say RSS*. N.p., n.d. Web. 21 Aug. 2014. <http://www.aim.org/wls/category/marriage/>.

"'Married couples report greater sexual satisfaction.' 'Married women report higher levels of physical and psychological health.' 'Married people are more likely to volunteer.' 'Being married increases the likelihood of affluence.' 'Married people tend to experience less depression and fewer problems with alcohol.' 'Getting married increases the probability of moving out of a poor neighborhood.' 'Married men make more money.' 'Ever-married women are less likely to experience poverty.' 'Marriage is associated with a lower mortality risk.'" "FamilyFacts.org." *The Benefits of Marriage*. The Heritage Foundation, n.d. Web. 05 Aug. 2014. <http://www.familyfacts.org/briefs/1/the-benefits-of-marriage>.

"single men, who were in good health, were 88% more likely to die throughout the course of the study" "The Benefits of Being Married." *Benefits of Marriage: Men's Health*. N.p., n.d. Web. 5 Aug. 2014. <http://www.menshealth.com/mhlists/benefits_of_marriage_and_ commitment/index.php?cm_mmc=MSN-_-Health-_-Can-love-be-unhealthy-_-benefits-of-marriage>.

"those who marry before 25 have a 50% higher divorce rate than those who marry older." "National Survey of Family Growth." *Centers for Disease Control and Prevention*. Centers for Disease Control and Prevention, 22 July 2015. Web. 8 Sept. 2016. <http://www.cdc.gov/nchs/nsfg/index.htm>.

147

**"whether the couple cohabitated before marriage, which increases risk of divorce significantly"** Jay, Meg. "The Downside of Cohabiting Before Marriage." *The New York Times*. The New York Times, 14 Apr. 2012. Web. 6 Aug. 2014.
<http://www.nytimes.com/2012/04/15/opinion/sunday/the-downside-of-cohabiting-before-marriage.html?pagewanted=all&_r=2&>.

**"couples who lived in poverty were far more likely to divorce, regardless of age."** Pear, Robert. "Poverty Termed a Divorce Factor." *Nytimes.com*. The New York Times Company, 15 Jan. 1993. Web. 8 Sept. 2016.
<http://www.nytimes.com/1993/01/15/us/poverty-termed-a-divorce-factor.html>.

**"the divorce rate for couples who remained completely abstinent until marriage is only *five percent*."** "Sex and Dating Advice for Teenagers - Mark Gungor." *YouTube*. YouTube, 27 Mar. 2014. Web. 05 Aug. 2014.
<https://www.youtube.com/watch?v=LbYTkGitMyk>.

**"in terms of longitude and happiness levels, the best time to marry is between the ages of 22-25."** Glenn, Norval D., Jeremy Uecker, and Robert Love W.B., Jr. "Later First Marriage and Marrital Success." *Http://www.ncbi.nlm.nih.gov*. National Center for Biotechnology Information, 10 June 2010. Web. 9 Sept. 2016.
<http://www.ncbi.nlm.nih.gov/pmc/articles/PMC3437253/>.

**"Median Marriage by Decade" (graph)** "Median Age at First Marriage, 1890–2010." *Infoplease.com*. Sandbox Networks, Inc., n.d. Web. 8 Sept. 2016. <http://www.infoplease.com/ipa/A0005044.html>.

**"the divorce rate has become steadily worse over the course of these decades."** "Marriages and Divorces, 1900–2012." *Infoplease.com*. Sandbox Networks, Inc., n.d. Web. 8 Sept. 2016.
<http://www.infoplease.com/ipa/A0005044.html>.

**"fun videos that will hold your attention much better than I could and will, hopefully, put your mind at ease about so-called overpopulation"** "Latest Video." *Overpopulation Is a Myth* |. N.p., n.d. Web. 17 Aug. 2014. <http://overpopulationisamyth.com/>.

**"'We tend to think economic growth comes from working harder and smarter.'"** "Dropping Birth Rates Threaten Global Economic Growth." *CBSNews*. CBS Interactive, 07 May. 2014. Web. 17 Aug. 2014. <http://www.cbsnews.com/news/dropping-birth-rates-threaten-global-economic-growth/>.

**"because we had the lowest birth rates in recorded history in 2012."** Kurtz, Annalyn. "U.S Birth Rate Falls to Record Low." *CNNMoney*. Cable News Network, 06 Sept. 2013. Web. 19 Aug. 2014. <http://money.cnn.com/2013/09/06/news/economy/birth-rate-low/>.

**"Currently, three full-time workers are required to support one Social Security recipient"** "Va. Senator Says Fewer Workers Supporting More Social Security Retirees." *PolitiFact Georgia.* Politifact.com, 11 Apr. 2011. Web. 21 Aug. 2014.
<http://www.politifact.com/georgia/statements/2011/apr/12/mark-warner/va-senator-says-fewer-workers-supporting-more-soci/>.

**"we need almost three full-time workers for every Medicare recipient..."** "The Number of Workers per Medicare Beneficiary Is Falling." *The Heritage Foundation.* The Heritage Foundation, 22 May. 2012. Web. 21 Aug. 2014.
<http://www.heritage.org/multimedia/infographic/2012/05/medicare-at-risk/the-number-of-workers-per-medicare-beneficiary-is-falling>.

**"Japan actually had more deaths than births in 2012."** Usatoday. "As U.S. Birth Rate Drops, Concern for the Future Mounts." *USA Today.* Gannett, 13 Feb. 2013. Web. 19 Aug. 2014.
<http://www.usatoday.com/story/news/nation/2013/02/12/us-births-decline/1880231/>.

**"their population is shrinking by one citizen every one hundred seconds and, if they are to continue at this rate, their entire population would be extinct in just 1,000 years."** Oliver, Amy. "Falling Birth Rates Mean Japan 'won't Have Any Children under 15 by 3011'" *Mail Online.* Associated Newspapers, 13 May 2012. Web. 19 Aug. 2014. <http://www.dailymail.co.uk/news/article-2143748/Falling-birth-rates-mean-Japan-wont-children-15-3011-current-trend-continues.html>.

**"husbands and wives who share household work had a 50% higher divorce rate than those where the woman shouldered most of it." "'Maybe it's sometimes seen as a good thing to have very clear roles with lots of clarity.'"** Samuel, Henry. "Couples Who Share the Housework Are More Likely to Divorce, Study Finds." *The Telegraph.* Telegraph Media Group, 27 Sept. 2012. Web. 21 Aug. 2014.
<http://www.telegraph.co.uk/news/worldnews/europe/9572187/Couples-who-share-the-housework-are-more-likely-to-divorce-study-finds.html>.

**"unrealistic Enjoli perfume ad from the 80s called 'The 24 Hour Woman'"** "Enjoli - 1980." *YouTube.* YouTube, 7 Jul. 2009. Web. 21 Aug. 2014. <https://www.youtube.com/watch?v=jA4DR4vEgrs>

THE WAR ON MEN:

**"'...[B]eing a mother isn't really work...'"** Wurtzel, Elizabeth. "1% Wives Are Helping Kill Feminism and Make the War on Women Possible." *The Atlantic.* Atlantic Media Company, 15 June 2012.

Web. 20 Aug. 2014.
<http://www.theatlantic.com/politics/archive/2012/06/1-wives-are-helping-kill-feminism-and-make-the-war-on-women-possible/258431/2/>.

**"'Being a housewife is an illegitimate profession...'"** "Vivian Gornick." *Wikipedia*. Wikimedia Foundation, 11 Jun. 2007. Web. 20 Aug. 2014. <http://en.wikipedia.org/wiki/Vivian_Gornick>.

**"'[Housewives] are dependent creatures who are still children...parasites.'"** "LAF/Beautiful Womanhood» "You Don't Know Feminism"." *LAFBeautiful Womanhood RSS*, 20 Mar. 2010. Web. 20 Aug. 2014. <http://www.ladiesagainstfeminism.com/theme-articles/you-dont-know-feminism/>.

**"'A parasite sucking out the living strength of another organism...'"** "Feminism (Quotations)." - *WikiMANNia*. N.p., 30 Jul. 2011. Web. 22 Aug. 2014. <http://en.wikimannia.org/Feminism_(Quotations)>.

**"The male is a domestic animal which, if treated with firmness... can be trained to do most things."** "Jilly Cooper Quote." *BrainyQuote*. Xplore, n.d. Web. 19 Aug. 2014. <http://www.brainyquote.com/quotes/quotes/j/jillycoope172702.html>.

**"'Men are rapists, batterers, plunderers, killers...'"** "Talk:Andrea Dworkin." - *Conservapedia*. N.p., n.d. Web. 20 Aug. 2014. <http://www.conservapedia.com/Talk%3AAndrea_Dworkin>.

**"'I feel that 'man-hating' is an honourable and viable political act...'"** "Robin Morgan." - *Wikiquote*. N.p., n.d. Web. 20 Aug. 2014. <http://en.wikiquote.org/wiki/Robin_Morgan>.

**"'As long as some men use physical force to subjugate females, all men need not.'"** "Quotations about Feminism." - *Conservapedia*. N.p., n.d. Web. 20 Aug. 2014. <http://www.conservapedia.com/Quotations_about_Feminism>.

**"'The proportion of men must be reduced to and maintained at approximately 10% of the human race.'"** "Humanity Should Be 10% Male 90% Female (BC Prof Mary Daly)." *Humanity Should Be 10% Male 90% Female (BC Prof Mary Daly)*. N.p., 28 Nov. 2002. Web. 20 Aug. 2014. <http://www.freerepublic.com/focus/news/797534/posts>.

**"Four times as many scholarships specifically for women."** Ny, Rachel. "4x As Many Scholarships for Women - a Disadvantage for Men?" *NerdWallet*, NerdWallet, 11 May 2017, www.nerdwallet.com/blog/loans/student-loans/4x-scholarships-women/.

**"More women than men have been attending college since the 1970s"** CCAP Contributor. "The Male-Female Ratio in Col-

lege." *Forbes*, Forbes Magazine, 16 Feb. 2012,
www.forbes.com/sites/ccap/2012/02/16/the-male-female-
ratio-in-college/#55d7af1fa52d.

"boys are five times more likely than girls to be expelled from pre-
school ..." "boys account for about 70% of all suspensions."
"seven-year-old Maryland boy named Josh Welch was sent
home from school for biting a Pop Tart into the shape of a
gun." "Boys generally receive lower grades, win fewer honors,
and are less likely to go to college." War on Boys. Perf. Christina
Hoff Sommers. YouTube. Prager University, 19 May 2014. Web. 10
Sept. 2016. <https://www.youtube.com/watch?v=OFpYj0E-yb4>.

"nearly 20% of all American boys are diagnosed with ADHD..."
D'Agostino, Ryan. "The Drugging of the American Boy." Esquire.
Hearst Communications, Inc., 24 Feb. 2015. Web. 9 Sept. 2016.
<http://www.esquire.com/news-politics/a32858/drugging-of-the-
american-boy-
0414/?click=smart&kw=ist&src=smart&mag=ESQ&link=http%3A
%2F%2Fwww.esquire.com%2Ffeatures%2Fdrugging-of-the-
american-boy-0414>.

"boys are less organized, less attentive, perform worse socially than
girls, and boys are less likely to ask a question on a subject
they don't understand." "'The social and behavioral skills gap
between boys and girls...'" Mchaney, Sarah. "How Do We Help
Boys Close the Academic Gender Gap?" PBS. PBS, 7 May 2014.
Web. 13 Sept. 2016.
<http://www.pbs.org/newshour/updates/classroom-rigged-
boys/>.

"'Bumbling Dad' TV tropes" "Bumbling Dad." *TV Tropes*,
tvtropes.org/pmwiki/pmwiki.php/Main/BumblingDad.

"Mansplain" "Words We're Watching: Mansplaining." Merriam-
webster.com. Merriam-Webster Incorporated, n.d. Web. 10 Sept.
2016.

"'This is a controversial idea and one that many people are reluctant
to talk about for fear of appearing sexist.'" "Anxiety Disorders
on Rise Among Women." Promises Addiction Treatment Alcohol
Drug Rehab Malibu. Promises Treatment Centers, 14 Aug. 2013.
Web. 20 Aug. 2014. <http://www.promises.com/articles/mental-
health/are-women-wired-to-worry/>.

THE CASE FOR WOMEN TO BE HOMEMAKERS:

"'The homemaker has the ultimate career...'" "A Quote by C.S. Lewis." *Goodreads*. N.p., n.d. Web. 16 Aug. 2014.
<https://www.goodreads.com/quotes/20606-the-homemaker-has-
the-ultimate-career-all-other-careers-exist>.

**"69.9% of all mothers work outside the home" "57.3% of mothers with infant children work outside the home"** "Latest Annual Data." *Women's Bureau (WB)*. U.S. Department of Labor, 2013. Web. 16 Aug. 2014.
<http://www.dol.gov/wb/stats/recentfacts.htm#age>.

**"'Upon reviewing studies of maternal employment and of nonparental care...'"** Belsky, Jay, and David Eggebeen. "Early and Extensive Maternal Employment and Young Children's Socioemotional Development: Children of the National Longitudinal Survey of Youth." *JSTOR.org*. Pennsylvania State University, 4 Nov. 1991. Web. 18 Aug. 2014.
<http://www.jstor.org/discover/10.2307/353011?uid=3739928&uid=2&uid=4&uid=3739256&sid=21104551924627>.

**"'The results differed by gender, an effect also seen in humans...'" "'shows that early life conditions critically affect adult health. Maternal attachment plays a fundamental role in shaping who we are; remove it and the harm is great.'" "'The longer these children were left in their cribs, simply being fed...'"** Szalavitz, Maia, and Maia Szalavitz. "The Measure of a Mother's Love: How Early Deprivation Derails Child Development." *Time*. Time, 24 May. 2012. Web. 22 Aug. 2014.
<http://healthland.time.com/2012/05/24/the-measure-of-a-mothers-love-how-early-deprivation-derails-child-development/>.

**"Back in the 1940s, when autism was first being discovered, the term "refrigerator mother" was coined."** "Refrigerator Mother." *Wikipedia*. Wikimedia Foundation, 29 Apr. 2005. Web. 13 Aug. 2014.
<http://en.wikipedia.org/wiki/Refrigerator_mother>.

**"Bruno Bettelheim, who performed studies about autism being linked to a lack of affection"** "Bruno Bettelheim." *Wikipedia*. Wikimedia Foundation, 07 May. 2004. Web. 17 Aug. 2014.
<http://en.wikipedia.org/wiki/Bruno_Bettelheim>.

**"the 78% increase in autism in the past twelve years"** Falco, Miriam. "CDC: U.S. Kids with Autism up 78% in past Decade." *CNN*. Cable News Network, 29 Mar. 2012. Web. 10 Aug. 2014.
<http://www.cnn.com/2012/03/29/health/autism/>.

**"the 30% increase in just the past two ."** Falco, Miriam. "Autism Rates Now 1 in 68 U.S. Children: CDC." *CNN*. Cable News Network, 28 Mar. 2014. Web. 19 Aug. 2014.
<http://www.cnn.com/2014/03/27/health/cdc-autism/>.

**"a recent HealthDay News study that shows adult autism patients benefited greatly from the hormone oxytocin"** "'Love Hormone' Oxytocin May Help Some With Autism." *Consumer HealthDay*. HealthDay, 29 Jul. 2014. Web. 22 Aug. 2014.
<http://consumer.healthday.com/cognitive-health-information-

26/autism-news-51/love-hormone-oxytocin-may-help-some-with-autism-690156.html>.

**"The impacts of neglect can result in anti-social behaviors, delinquency, teenage pregnancy, depression, anxiety, self-esteem issues, etc."** "Child Neglect: A Guide for Prevention, Assessment and Intervention." *Impact of Neglect.* U.S. Department of Health and Human Services, 2006. Web. 14 Aug. 2014.
<https://www.childwelfare.gov/pubs/usermanuals/neglect/chapterthree.cfm>.

**"In 2010, women comprised about 47% of the total labor force."** "Women's Bureau (WB) - Quick Facts on Women in the Labor Force in 2010." *Women's Bureau (WB) - Quick Facts on Women in the Labor Force in 2010.* U.S. Department of Labor, 2010. Web. 14 Aug. 2014. <http://www.dol.gov/wb/factsheets/Qf-laborforce-10.htm>.

**Women in the Workforce Increases vs. Household Income Increases Graph:** Indicator. *16. Median Family Income* (n.d.): n. pag. Web.
<http://nces.ed.gov/pubs98/yi/yi16.pdf>.
"United States Census Bureau." *Historical Income Tables.* U.S. Department of Commerce, n.d. Web. 19 Aug. 2014.
<https://www.census.gov/hhes/www/income/data/historical/household/>.
*Infoplease.* Infoplease, n.d. Web. 20 Aug. 2014.
<http://www.infoplease.com/ipa/A0104673.html>.

**Men's Pay vs Women's Pay:** "United States Census Bureau." *Historical Income Tables.* U.S. Department of Commerce, n.d. Web. 23 Aug. 2014.
<http://www.census.gov/hhes/www/income/data/historical/people/>.

**"the 2002 romantic comedy, My Big Fat Greek Wedding..."** "2002 Film by Joel Zwick." *Albert Einstein - Wikiquote,* Wikimedia Foundation, Inc., 25 Apr. 2018,
en.wikiquote.org/wiki/My_Big_Fat_Greek_Wedding.

**"This is becoming so widespread that there's actually a term for it: the 'work spouse.'"** "Work Spouse." *Wikipedia.* Wikimedia Foundation, 16 May. 2006. Web. 20 Aug. 2014.
<http://en.wikipedia.org/wiki/Work_spouse>.
"Dr. Phil.com - Advice - How to Keep Boundaries with a "Work Spouse"" *Dr. Phil.com - Advice - How to Keep Boundaries with a "Work Spouse"* Peteski Productions, n.d. Web. 20 Aug. 2014.
<http://www.drphil.com/articles/article/693>.
*CNN.* Cable News Network, n.d. Web. 23 Aug. 2014.
<http://www.cnn.com/2008/LIVING/worklife/11/10/cb.seven.signs.work.spouse/index.html?eref=rss_us>.

Chun, Janean. "Signs You've Crossed The Line With Your Work Spouse." *The Huffington Post.* TheHuffingtonPost.com, 26 Sept. 2012. Web. 20 Aug. 2014.
<http://www.huffingtonpost.com/2012/09/26/work-spouse_n_1901577.html>.

Feature, Heather HatfieldWebMD. "The Office Spouse: Rules of Engagement."*WebMD.* WebMD, n.d. Web. 23 Aug. 2014.
<http://www.webmd.com/sex-relationships/features/the-office-spouse-rules-of-engagement>.

**"65% of women find an emotional affair more hurtful than a sexual affair."** Ledbetter, Sheri. "Chapman University Publishes Research on Jealousy – Impact of Sexual vs. Emotional Infidelity." *Blogs.chapman.edu10.* Chapman University, 5 Jan. 2015. Web. 13 Sept. 2016. <https://blogs.chapman.edu/press-room/2015/01/05/chapman-university-publishes-research-on-jealousy-impact-of-sexual-vs-emotional-infidelity/>.

**"suicide rates are up for both middle-aged genders, a 40% increase from 1999 to 2010, women now attempt suicide three times as often as men"** "Dramatic Rise In Suicide Rate Among Middle-Aged Women - CBS Miami."*CBS Miami.* CBS Local Media, 7 Jun. 2013. Web. 20 Aug. 2014.
<http://miami.cbslocal.com/2013/06/07/dramatic-rise-in-suicide-rate-among-middle-aged-women/>.

**"Countries where women have the most opportunities are also the countries with the most alcoholism and drug abuse among women"** "Addiction's Shrinking Gender Gap | The Fix." *The Fix.* The Fix, 7 Mar. 2013. Web. 19 Aug. 2014.
<http://www.thefix.com/content/addiction-global-gender-gap-women-equal-opportunity8151>.

**"'Conflicts between family and work influenced depression risk for both sexes, but in different ways…'"** "On-the-Job Depression Study Highlights Gender Boundaries for Men and Women." *Forbes.* Forbes Magazine, 10 May. 2012. Web. 23 Aug. 2014.
<http://www.forbes.com/sites/shenegotiates/2012/05/10/on-the-job-depression-study-highlights-gender-boundaries-for-men-and-women/>.

**"'…[W]omen in the United States have become less happy, both absolutely and relative to men.'" "'…[T]rends in self-reported subjective well-being indicate that happiness has shifted to-ward men…'" "'Finally, the changes brought about through the women's movement may have decreased women's happi-ness.'"** Stevenson, Betsey, and Justin Wolfers. "The Paradox of the Declining Female Happiness." *Nber.org.* National Bureau of Economic Research, May 2009. Web. 18 Aug. 2014.
<http://www.nber.org/papers/w14969.pdf?new_window=1>.

**"The Feminists did not look ... far [enough] ahead"** "Moon Shell." *Gift from the Sea,* by Anne M. Lindbergh, Pantheon, 1955, pp. 50–51.

**"from 2000 to 2009, the number of women incarcerated increased over 20% compared an increase of about 15% for men"** Ajinkya, Julie. "Rethinking How to Address the Growing Female Prison Population." *Center For American Progress.* Center For American Progress, 8 Mar. 2013. Web. 24 Aug. 2014.
<http://www.americanprogress.org/issues/women/news/2013/03/08/55787/rethinking-how-to-address-the-growing-female-prison-population/>.

**"'When the real history of mankind is fully disclosed, will it feature the echoes of gunfire or the shaping sound of lullabies?...'"** Maxwell, Neal A. "The Women of God." *Lds.org.* N.p., Apr. 1978. Web. 19 Aug. 2014. <https://www.lds.org/general-conference/1978/04/the-women-of-god?lang=eng>.

**"'The world has enough women who are tough; we need women who are tender...'"** Nadauld, Margaret D. "The Joy of Womanhood." *Lds.org.* N.p., Oct. 2000. Web. 19 Aug. 2014. <https://www.lds.org/general-conference/2000/10/the-joy-of-womanhood?lang=eng>.

FEMINIST FAIRY TALE: CHIEF EXECUTIVE PRINCESS:

**"It's the true story of Indra Nooyi, CEO of PepsiCo"** "Success Story: Indra Nooyi | MBARendezvous.com." *Success Story: Indra Nooyi | MBARendezvous.com.* N.p., n.d. Web. 23 Aug. 2014.
<http://www.mbarendezvous.com/motivation-story-indra-nooyi-22.asp>.

**"'I don't think women can have it all. I just don't think so...'" "'My observation... is that the biological clock and the career clock are in total conflict with each other...'" "'The person who hurts the most through this whole thing is your spouse...'"** Friedersdorf, Conor. "Why PepsiCo CEO Indra K. Nooyi Can't Have It All." *The Atlantic.* Atlantic Media Company, 01 July 2014. Web. 17 Aug. 2014.
<http://www.theatlantic.com/business/archive/2014/07/why-pepsico-ceo-indra-k-nooyi-cant-have-it-all/373750/>.

# ABOUT THE AUTHORS

Danelle and Kylie Malchus are a mother and daughter writing duo from Murray, Utah who pretend to love each other in public sometimes. Most days, when they're not working, writing, painting, or discussing politics, they're spending their time binge-watching cult shows on Netflix with the other daughter.

Join the ever-growing "End Feminism" movement and keep up with current events at:
WWW.FACEBOOK.COM/END FEMINISMSAVETHEWORLD